TELEPEN
D0487810

JULY 23. 1762.

MEMORIAL

FOR THE

COLLIERS of *Scotland*.

CONSIDERING the Poverty, the Ignorance, and the ſequeſtered State of the Memorialiſts, it could not be expected, that a Spirit of Liberty ſhould reach them, as ſoon as the reſt of their Fellow Subjects: Hence it was, that when the *Britiſh* Legiſlature was diſpoſed to enfranchize the People of this Country as much as poſſible, when the wiſe and ſalutary Laws, aboliſhing Ward-holdings and heritable Juriſdictions, were enacted; no Perſon appeared to repreſent the hard Condition of the Memorialiſts, ſo that, whilſt Independence was conferred on others, their Bondage was continued.

But Knowledge gain'd Ground daily, and the Irradiations of Liberty have at laſt penetrated even to the Memorialiſts. They are now ſenſible what the Sweets of Liberty muſt be; and, as the Reaſons of Expediency and public Utility, which were made the Pretexts for enſlaving them, have long ago ceaſed, they are perſuaded no Perſon of Candour, or Humanity, will blame them for exerting themſelves to the utmoſt, to obtain their Freedom.

With this View, the Memorialiſts laid their Caſe before the ableſt Council, both in *England* and *Scotland:* And being adviſed, that an Application to the Legiſlature was their proper Remeedy, they have contributed a Sum ſufficient to defray

Memorial for the Colliers of Scotland
for abolition of serfdom (1762)
(page 2)

A SHORT HISTORY OF

LABOUR IN SCOTLAND

W. H. MARWICK, M.A.

W. & R. CHAMBERS LTD.
11 THISTLE STREET, EDINBURGH
AND LONDON

Printed in Great Britain by
T. & A. Constable Limited
Hopetoun Street, Edinburgh

CONTENTS

ACKNOWLEDGMENTS

THE author and publishers make grateful acknowledgment to the following who provided illustrations for this book:

The Trustees of the National Library of Scotland for The Memorial for the Colliers of Scotland; Membership Card of West of Scotland Power Loom Female Weavers' Society; and Workmen's Co-operative Dwellings.

The Town Clerk, the Burgh of Kilsyth and Mr John Watson for the Banners of 1832 Reform Bill agitation, and Mr C. S. Minto, Edinburgh City Librarian, for the photograph of Hugh Miller Place, looking North.

FOREWORD

INTEREST in the history of the Scottish Labour movement is comparatively recent, but has rapidly increased. As a subject of academic study, its origin may be assigned to the publication seventy years ago of the Webbs' *History of Trade Unionism* (1894), which contains Scottish references. Since then, by the efforts of writers of whom G. D. H. Cole is best known, a considerable number of works dealing with the British movement have been produced. A specially Scottish contribution emerged withThomas Johnston's *History of the Working Classes in Scotland* and William Stewart's *Life of Keir Hardie* in the early 1920's.

Within the last few years, interest both in academic and in trade union circles has been stimulated by the activities of the Society for the Study of Labour History. Its Scottish Committee has compiled an extensive bibliography of material, much of which was hitherto unknown. A course on the History of the Working Class Movement was given for ten years in the University of Edinburgh, and a centre has been established at the University of Strathclyde. Several scholars are pursuing research on the subject.

It therefore seems appropriate that a short survey of what is already known (such as, apart from my own booklet of 1948, has not hitherto appeared) should be published, designed to appeal both to students and to the general reader interested in the origin and growth of what is now a major factor in our public life. It suffers from the meagreness of early records, usually formal and jejune, while other contemporary references are often ill-informed and prejudiced.

W. H. MARWICK

ABBREVIATIONS

In accordance with common practice, and to economise space, initials are normally utilised in reference to the following bodies:

A.S.E.	Amalgamated Society of Engineers.
A.S.R.S.	Amalgamated Society of Railway Servants.
G.F.T.U.	General Federation of Trade Unions.
I.L.P.	Independent Labour Party.
M.F.G.B.	Miners Federation of Great Britain.
N.C.L.C.	National Council of Labour Colleges.
N.U.C.	National Union of Clerks.
N.U.R.	National Union of Railwaymen.
S.C.W.S.	Scottish Cooperative Wholesale Society.
S.D.F.	Social Democratic Federation.
T.G.W.U.	Transport and General Workers Union.
T.U.C.	Trades Union Congress.
W.E.A.	Workers Educational Association.
W.E.T.U.C.	Workers Educational Trade Union Committee.

CHAPTER I

ENVIRONMENT AND MOTIVE FORCES

THE industrialisation of Scotland was relatively late and rapid. Its natural resources remained largely unexploited until the late eighteenth century—the prevalence of internal and external strife was a chief inhibiting factor—but recent study has demonstrated some advance in the late sixteenth and early seventeenth centuries, especially in coal-mining. Retarded by the Civil War, industrial growth on mercantilist principles was promoted by the Restoration Government, when such enterprises as the weaving of woollen cloth, soap-boiling and ropemaking developed. Clandestinely, or by special licence, some part was obtained in colonial trade. The 'Disaster of Darien' and the famine years in the 1690's dislocated the economy, and probably facilitated acceptance of the Union of 1707.

The economic consequences of the Union are still a matter of acute controversy; there is some warrant for the view that, for good or ill, they have been exaggerated. The woollen and other industries such as salt refining suffered from competition, and the burden of taxation was increased. On the other hand there were gains to Scotland, chief of which were the growth of the export of cattle to England and the opening of the American trade, exchanging tobacco and sugar for manufactured products. The profits of both, and of improved agricultural techniques, provided capital for industrial investment, contributed to also by the 'Equivalent' grant of Parliamentary funds by the Treaty, administered from 1728 by the Board of Manufactures. Other factors favouring economic progress included the study of physics and chemistry and their industrial application, the cessation of civic conflict, save for the episodes of the '15 and '45, the growth of a flexible banking system, the comparatively high standard of popular education, and perhaps the secularisation of interests between the Covenanting era and the Disruption struggle.

The expansion of coal-mining, the establishment of ironworks, the beginning of a factory system, at first associated with water power, in the native textiles (wool and linen) and especially in the novel and exotic cotton, and the construction of canals, mark the first stage of the 'industrial revolution' in the latter part of the eighteenth century. Old handicraft industries survived, usually regulated by the gilds or 'incorporations'; but their control weakened, with the grant of exemptions and the spread of industry outwith burghal bounds. Though their powers were not abolished until 1846, the incorporations tended to become property-holding bodies divorced from industry. The social tradition that was more potent in the newer industries was that of paternalism. Coal-mines, ironworks, salt-refineries and timber-mills were in many cases incidental to the management of a landed estate, or leased on the same principle as agricultural farms. The coal-miners were reduced to what virtually became hereditary serfdom by legislation of the early seventeenth century; the rapid expansion of the industry in the west made this system increasingly uneconomic, and legal emancipation was finally achieved in 1799, though long-term contracts of service remained frequent.

Regulation of conditions of labour, especially wages, was imitated from the Elizabethan Act of Artificers, in the powers given to magistrates by an Act of 1617, re-enacted in 1661. One clause of the latter statute instructed J.P.s that they 'shall have power to decerne and compell the master to make payment of the fees . . . in caice the servants please rather to pursu for the same befor them than any other judge'. Dr. C. A. Malcolm's investigation of the Minutes of the J.P.s for Lanarkshire (Scottish History Society, 1931) shows that in the early eighteenth century the wages of masons, wrights, thatchers, labourers, barrowmen and farm servants were settled by the Justices, and revised annually at the August Quarter Sessions. The sum fixed was a maximum, not to be exceeded under penalty of a fine. Saddlers, shoemakers, blacksmiths, lorimers, and linen workers were excluded. A decision given by the Dumfriesshire J.P.s in 1751 indicates the application of the law to agricultural labourers.

The political structure was even less democratic than south of the Border. The pre-Union basis of the Estates was preserved in Scottish representation in the House of Commons. Burgh representatives were normally 'elected' by nominees of the local councils, usually in groups, while these 'Royal Burghs' were themselves in most cases governed by councils nominated by the Merchant Gilds and Craft Incorporations; the method encouraged bribery and intimidation. Hence burgh reform was the prime demand of the agitation of the 1780's. County representatives were chosen on a very restricted and antiquated basis of landholding; fictitious qualifications were frequently created by landowners for electoral purposes. The French Revolution stimulated the activities of Thomas Muir and the other 'Political Martyrs' sentenced to transportation by the notorious Braxfield. Some support by skilled workers, especially of the more extreme 'United Scotsmen' (1796-97), is indicated. Colliers are said to have been much involved in the riots provoked by the Militia Act of 1797—notably at Tranent.

Unrest died down during the Napoleonic Wars, but it was revived after Waterloo, encouraged by post-war depression as well as by the propaganda of Cartwright, Hunt and Cobbett. Some prosecutions on the ground of sedition were instituted, but the chief suspects, Rev. Neil Douglas, an eccentric and heretical clergyman, and Andrew McKinlay, a weaver, were acquitted. The movement culminated in the fiasco of the 'Radical Rising' of 1820, sometimes regarded as the work of *agents provocateurs*, such as Alexander Richmond, a leader of the weavers in 1812 but now associated with Lord Provost Kirkman Finlay of Glasgow, a commercial magnate; his *Narrative of the Condition of the Manufacturing Population* (1824), a useful contemporary survey, is in part his apologia and exculpation. A manifesto of a Provisional Government Committee, calling for a general strike, was widely placarded in the Glasgow area, perhaps appropriately on 1st April. Some 60,000 are said to have participated, but returned to work in a few days. A small group set out, apparently to capture the Carron ironworks, but were dispersed at Bonnybridge by the yeomanry; some casualties occurred in a riot at Greenock. Three artisans were executed as ringleaders—Wilson, Baird and Hardie, the last sometimes mistakenly claimed as a forebear of Keir Hardie. John Parkhill (1787-1861), who later wrote *Reminiscenses* under the name of 'Arthur Sneddon' and was a critic of Chartism, and John Henderson, ironmonger, who was also implicated, escaped to America; the latter, nicknamed 'Cutler Jock', was later editor of a Radical paper, became provost of Paisley and a 'convinced' member of the Society of Friends. John Fraser of Johnstone, afterwards a Chartist leader, was imprisoned, but released after three months without trial.

Chapter II

THE ORIGINS OF TRADE UNIONISM

It is now realised that organisations that can be classed as trade unions existed before the era commonly designated the Industrial Revolution, though through the lack of records our knowledge of them is fragmentary, and derived from casual references. The continuity of the trade union with the gild has long been refuted; but it is clear that the nascent unions were imitative, particularly in their insistence on craft regulations and attempts to enforce a monopoly of labour, and in their provision of 'friendly benefits'. Eighteenth-century illustrations of such 'unions' include the Journeymen Coopers of Glasgow (1752), the Dundee Baxters and the Hawick Stockingmakers. Workers thus associated for self-help in providing against the risks of life could hardly ignore their common interest in their conditions of employment. Industrial and 'friendly' aims were sometimes not clearly demarcated, especially when overt trade union activity incurred legal penalties. Some employers, particularly in coal-mining, anticipated American 'company unionism' by fostering the association of their own employees for 'mutual benefit' purposes. In a few older industries the rudiments of trade unionism may be traced to the recurrent disputes between journeymen, who were without prospect of becoming independent masters, and the ruling oligarchies within the incorporation.

Probably, however, a chief element is to be found in the casual and spontaneous gathering of a body of workers, congregated in employment and residence, who in the attempt to redress concrete grievances came to realise the potential strength of numbers and unity. Time and again a more or less permanent society emerges from joint action in a dispute—e.g. handloom weavers, mainly scattered in 'domestic' industry.

Information about these early unions comes largely from the legal cases in which they were involved. That relating to the tailoring trade is the most copious. A strike of journeymen tailors for advance of wages took place in Edinburgh in 1748. The strikers were indicted at the instance of the Incorporation of Tailors, and under threat of heavy penalty were compelled to 'enact not to be guilty in future'. Ten years later the journeymen applied to the Edinburgh magistrates for an hour's reduction in the working day and for increased wages. Edinburgh and Canongate Incorporations united in carrying resistance to this project as far as the Court of Session, with eventual success. In 1762 the Court approved the local finding that 'the arts and manufactures which are necessary to the wellbeing of society must be subjected to rules. This power has long been exercised by the magistrates of burghs and J.P.s, under review of the sovereign court.' A maximum wage of a shilling a day was confirmed, and penalties imposed for refusal to work on these terms. A similar ruling was given in July 1778.

About this date, the journeymen are described as holding weekly meetings in 'clubhouses', and levying dues on all employees, in order to exert pressure on the masters. The Incorporations of Edinburgh and neighbourhood therefore collaborated in setting up a 'house of call' under their own control, and insisting on non-unionism. A committee was appointed to secure enforcement, by judicial process if necessary. Lukewarmness in application was however apparent, and Canongate members declined to assist their Edinburgh colleagues (or competitors) in further legal proceedings.

In Aberdeen also, journeymen tailors made an 'illegal combination' to raise wages in 1768, and indulged in a strike in 1797. Among casual references to other trades may be cited the existence of an Aberdeen Wrights' Society in 1732, the formation in 1755 by the journeymen woolcombers of Aberdeen of a society, which on appeal to the Court of Session was declared illegal, and the ship carpenters of Leith (1802), journeymen printers of Edinburgh (1803-04) and journeymen booksellers of Edinburgh (1811), in all of which cases the validity of judicial fixation of wages was vindicated.

In effect then, the law was invoked by employers, usually with success, to thwart demands for improved conditions. Attempts were made, as we shall see, by early trade unions to utilise this judicial procedure to their own advantage, ultimately without avail.

A divergence in the standpoint of English and Scots law may be worth noting at this point. 'By Scots Common Law,' says Professor Rankine, 'every company is a distinct persona'; i.e. Scots law was more ready to recognise the personality of an artificial group, whereas English law had an individualistic bias. Hence the legal status of such bodies as trade unions in respect, for example, of holding property was more readily accepted in Scotland. The *Scottish Journal of Jurisprudence*, with reference to contemporary cases, remarked in 1873 (basing its opinion on the eighteenth-century *Commentaries* of Baron Hume) that the technical difficulty found in England in punishing violations of rights of property of a union by its members or officers, arising from their being joint owners, does not arise in Scotland.

Another legal point of much concern to trade unions was the question of liability to prosecution for combination or 'conspiracy'. Here also some difference is apparent between the Scottish and English standpoint. English Common Law regarded as 'unlawful' societies operating 'in restraint of trade', and trade unions were deemed within this category; it also made their activities liable to be held criminal conspiracies. It is now held that the notorious Combination Laws of 1799, preceded as they were by enactments relating to particular trades, merely provided by statute more convenient procedural methods of dealing with such offences.

Scots Common Law appears to have been ambiguous in relation to combination. As Sheriff-substitute Campbell stated before the Select Committee on Artisans of 1824, 'the law of Scotland was rather undetermined with regard to combination'. J. L. Gray, after a review of contemporary evidence, concluded that the Combination Laws were not in fact applied in Scotland. In the main, the action taken against trade unions—as in the trial of journeymen paper-makers in Edinburgh in 1808—was based on a constructive interpretation of common as distinct from statute law. This interpretation hardened against them as organisation became more prevalent and suspect; and 'illustrates at once the change in the industrial situation and the impact of economic doctrine on the minds of the Scottish judges'. The 'McKimmie case' of 1813, arising out of the weavers' strike of the preceding year, is cited as the crucial indication of this new attitude; in effect, 'simple combination was declared illegal'. The *Edinburgh Review* of January 1824, giving examples of conflicting verdicts, concludes: 'Thus did the law of Scotland, having the power to declare new offences, vibrate between combination effected by great violence being no crime at all, and its being a crime when effected by simple union, even without any striking whatever'.

The prevalence of friendly societies, which on the other hand received legal protection, is attested by frequent references. In the parish of Old or West Monkland (Lanarkshire) there existed about 1800 a Society of 400 weavers who 'all work to the manufacturers of Glasgow'; it was 'governed by deacons and masters, to assist members in distress'. In Eastwood (Renfrewshire) there were later three friendly societies, the oldest dating from 1789. The annual subscription was 4s.; benefits included 'bedfast aliment' of 3s. per week, 'walking aliment' 2s. 1d. and superannuation of 2s. 1d. and 1s. 3d. There was a similar benefit society at Kilbarchan. The Ogleface Society (Stirlingshire) was perhaps unique in supplying a hearse for funerals of members.

The existence of spasmodic combinations of more militant type is demonstrated by occasional publicity. In June 1787 Glasgow weavers combined against a reduction in pay, agitated on Glasgow Green, and removed or smashed webs of non-strikers. They continued on strike until October. On 3rd September several strikers were killed by the military in a riot, and ringleaders were arrested. Of these, James Granger (1750-1825) was sentenced under Common Law to be whipped and banished for seven years; and the union was dissolved. The tombs of the victims in Calton Cemetery, Edinburgh, were restored in 1931 by Glasgow Trades Council, which published a brochure describing the episode.

A 'table of prices'—i.e. piecework rates—was adopted by leading houses in 1793, but was never uniform, and deviations took place progressively. The handloom weavers, being predisposed to maintain their vested interest in the *status quo*, sought to utilise the existing judicial machinery in their own interests. In 1800 there was a project for a joint committee of employers and employed to regulate wages, with appeal to legal arbitration in case of non-agreement; this was rejected, on *laissez faire* grounds, by the Glasgow Chamber of Commerce. In 1803 Parliament passed Arbitration Acts providing, in case of disputes in the cotton trade, for the appointment of arbiters by the justices. On several occasions, notably in 1808, the Scottish weavers joined in a petition to Parliament to limit apprenticeship and fix a minimum wage, but a Parliamentary Committee reported against action. Glasgow weavers drew up lists and articles, stipulating seven years' apprenticeship, limitation of numbers, etc., which were submitted to the Lord Advocate (1810) and investigated by the Sheriff (1811), without any exception being taken.

This line of action culminated in the famous lawsuit of 1812, deliberately undertaken as a test-case by 1500 operatives against 40 employers. The Glasgow weavers sought fixation of rates by the J.P.s of Lanarkshire Lower Ward; wages were alleged to have fallen 40 per cent since 1792. The continued competence of Quarter Sessions to fix wages was upheld on appeal to the Court of Session (*Fulton* v. *Mutrie*, June 1812). The case for the Weavers was stated by Cockburn, the Whig advocate and author, who cited precedents and rebutted arguments that these applied only to the fixing of maxima for specified handicraft trades in particular areas; the defendants claimed that scattered home workers such as weavers did not come within the scope of seventeenth-century legislation. Thus fortified, the justices ultimately recognised a scale varying from 8s. to 20s. per week, but made no order to enforce it. The employers rejected the 'table' thus endorsed, and a general strike of some 40,000 weavers followed. After three weeks, the Strike Committee were, as already noted, arrested and imprisoned for the offence of 'combination'. Jeffrey and Cockburn were counsel for the defence, and secured a light sentence for Alexander Richmond, alleged to be subsequently a government spy, who was one of the accused, and impressed them by his 'talent and influence'. The result of this, and of similar attempts in England, was the repeal in 1813 of the enactments, specifically including the Scottish Acts, which empowered justices to fix wages.

Union action had henceforth to rely in the main on industrial pressure to maintain or improve wage standards. Weavers' organisation continued. District Committees had been formed throughout the country, with Central Committees in Glasgow, Paisley and Perth, of which the first at any rate held weekly delegate meetings between 1809 and 1812. They are said to have declined overtures from the Luddites, though having 'a regular communication with Associations in England'; but their activities and their association with Radicalism rendered them suspect, especially in the period of the 'Radical Rising'. This attitude is reflected in fictitious guise in *The Young South Country Weaver*, a didactic novel by Rev. Henry Duncan, the pioneer of Savings Banks; and in the melodramatically entitled *Love and Freedom* of the mid-Victorian journalist William Freeland, which is based largely on Peter Mackenzie's *Reminiscences* and other contemporary writings, and introduces some of the Weavers' leaders and other historical characters.

In September 1824, 71 delegates from Glasgow and district adopted a constitution of 23 articles, including five years' apprenticeship, an 'infirm' allowance, and quarterly conferences; an increasing membership was reported in the local branches, which levied a penny per week. There were some disturbances, due to interference with employees of blacklisted employers; illegalities were repudiated by the union; a strike due to a local grievance was followed by a general lockout. Next year, numbers and finance were diminishing, and at a meeting in July of 53 delegates, a proposal to undertake co-operative production through the association was negatived.

The general expansion of unionism in the early 'thirties stimulated hopes of revival. On 15th January 1834 some 300 delegates assembled in Glasgow, claiming to represent about 50,000 weavers throughout Scotland and also Northern Ireland, where many worked for Glasgow entrepreneurs. They passed resolutions in favour of the establishment of 'Boards of Trade' on the Spitalfields model, to fix minimum rates.

There are a few scattered references to local organisation in this decade. In May 1834 the Paisley Committee were unsuccessfully sued for wages by the organiser of a strike. A Lanarkshire local union obtained an agreed table of prices (December 1833); but in 1838, after an unsuccessful attempt to buy up the stock of 'revels' (an essential part of the equipment) and so control output, the union was broken up by the Duke of Hamilton, and its funds confiscated. In December 1842 was reported the death of Hugh Mackenzie, 'long General Secretary of the West of Scotland Weavers' Association'.

The Weavers had economic forces against them in the growing utilisation of the power loom; and their subsequent history is one of increasing misery. A vivid impression of the decline is given in the anonymous autobiography, *A Short Account of the*

Life and Hardships of a Glasgow Weaver (1834). In 1792 he received 9¼d. per ell, in 1826 only 1⅜d., making an average earning of 3s. 9d. per week. Having had in 1815 a furnished house and loom shop, and been then an active church member, he was reduced in 1826 to pawning; his loom and implements were impounded for rent, and he was kept from church by lack of clothes.

The Whig magnates, Sir John Maxwell of Pollok, M.P. for Paisley in 1832-34, and his son of the same name, M.P. for Lanarkshire in 1832-37, became the Parliamentary champions of the handloom weavers. The latter vainly promoted a bill to achieve their aim of Wages Boards. His only achievement was the appointment of Select Committees of Inquiry into the trade (1834-35), of which he was chairman. A fuller investigation was carried out by Special Commissioners (1838-41). The general verdict was that the condition of the weavers was irretrievable, though some organisation still existed in the 'sixties, and casual practice and sporadic revival of the art of the handloom has continued to the present day.

NEWER TYPES OF UNION

The cotton spinners took the place of the weavers, as both the more important and the more notorious section of the trade. They were chiefly factory workers, of a less settled and orderly as well as more unskilled type, frequently immigrants from the Highlands or Ireland—hence their proclivity to violent methods. Their union has been traced to 1806; according to Cockburn, it was 'the real mover of all combinations and strikes in the manufacturing districts of Scotland for about twenty years'. The union rose and fell more than once. It became conspicuous in 1810, when the employers sought to force a pledge of non-unionism ('bond of disavowal'). Between 1816 and 1824, excesses occurred spasmodically. After a general lockout in January 1824, the union collapsed, but was revived after the repeal of the Combination Laws. It survived with difficulty through the trade depression of the late 'twenties, and was represented at a conference in the Isle of Man in December 1829, when a Grand General Union of the United Kingdom was formed—to endure for a year.

John Watson, Photographer, Kilsyth

Banners of Reform Bill agitation

(page 16)

UNITED TO PROTECT

The Bearer

Has been admitted a Member of the

WEST OF SCOTLAND

Power Loom Femal Weavers Society

President

Treasurer

Secretary

Glasgow 22 March 1833 No.

Miller lithog.

National Library of Scotland

Membership Card of the
West of Scotland Power Loom Female Weavers Society
(page 9)

The Association of Operative Cotton Spinners of Glasgow has received much attention, and its powers at this period were probably exaggerated by contemporary opinion, for example that of the Factory Commissioners of 1833, who asserted that it had 'complete monopoly of labour', enforced by intimidation. Its own professed objects were to 'support prices and enable members to obtain a fair remuneration'. A delegate was appointed by each shop, and these held general meetings quarterly; a committee of twelve met weekly. Funds were paid in weekly instalments. Entry was restricted to 'piecers', who had served their time. Strikes had to be authorised by the delegate meeting. 'Idle' benefit and funeral money were paid. The union had 800 to 900 members; a strike fund of £2000 was raised, and also an emigration fund. The introduction of female labour was resisted, and is said to have been accepted only on condition of equal pay.

The union achieved notoriety through the *cause célèbre* of 1837-38. In April 1837 it called a strike against a reduction of wages enforced by employers in combination. Five leaders were arrested, and the strike collapsed owing to the exhaustion of funds (29th July). The arrested were acquitted on charges of conspiracy and murder, but received sentences of transportation for seven years on minor counts; the 'innocence of mere combination' was judicially reiterated. They were actually detained in the hulks at Woolwich, and eventually received a free pardon on the intercession of Lord Brougham and Wakley the Radical surgeon (June 1840). Their return home was exploited in the Chartist agitation, but the released men seem to have derived little material benefit from their lionising. Their chairman, Thomas Hunter (1798-1867), a native of Antrim, put their case in a pamphlet, *The Rights of Labour Defended.*

The union survived on peaceful lines, although much weakened; an attempt was made in November 1839 to make good the outlay on the strike. In 1840, a scale of prices known as 'McNaught's List' was agreed upon; its alteration led to strikes in 1854 and 1876.

The existence of a West of Scotland Power Loom Female Weavers' Society is attested by the discovery of the membership card of Ellen Richy, dated 22nd March 1833.

Calico printing, which was an important subsidiary trade, mainly localised in the southern suburbs of Glasgow, in the

B

Campsies area, and on the Leven in Dunbartonshire, bred a separate unionism. A union was formed about 1800. Employers in the Vale of Leven secured the imprisonment of operatives in 1803, but the union survived a declaration of illegality in 1812. In 1814, the existence of a paid secretary, and regular relationships with unions in Lancashire and Ireland, are noted. Considerable funds were accumulated, and a general 'turnout' occurred. Five leaders were prosecuted, and on failure to appear were 'outlawed' (December 1814); the 'unanimity and firmness' of the employers were commended. At Campsie there was for a time a powerful association, with an entry fee of £10, and a monthly levy of 1s. 6d.; it was ruined by an unsuccessful strike in 1834. Outrages were reported at the same time at Dalsholm Printfield near Glasgow. In the kindred industry of bleaching, a union was formed in Renfrewshire in 1822.

There appears to have been less organisation in the older and primarily 'domestic' linen manufacture. A sickness benefit society existed among factory workers at Kirkcaldy (*c.* 1830). A 'turnout' took place at Broadford Works, Aberdeen (one of the earliest mills), against a reduction, and a 'female union' was formed, which collapsed after about a month (March 1834). The dissolution of a local union in Dundee was publicly announced, at the demand of the employers, after an unsuccessful strike (July 1834).

Directly associated with the textile trades was the making of tools and machinery for use therein. An embryo engineering union is found in the Operative Turners and Shuttlemakers of Glasgow, organised in 1831 by Abram Duncan, a 'pirnmaker' and later Chartist leader; it waged unsuccessful strikes in 1833-34. A Journeymen Steam Engine Makers' Society existed in Greenock in the 1820's.

A United Nailmakers' Society of Glasgow was active in 1832, when it exhausted its funds by assisting other unions on strike; it was revived in 1841 by Con Murphy, an Irish immigrant associated with Chartism. A Friendly Ironmoulders' Society, dating from 1809, formed a Glasgow branch in 1823, but collapsed in 1826-27. The Scottish Ironmoulders' Friendly Society was formed in October 1830 by James Dunn, a cotton spinner; it became a trade society as the Ironmoulders' Union.

The building trades, whose *History* by Raymond Postgate

includes Scottish material, were among the largest and most important, expanded, as Clapham has shown, by the demands of industrial growth, though little affected in technique or organisation, remaining small-scale handicrafts. They proved particularly susceptible to Owenite projects, perhaps because of the relatively small requirement of fixed capital. In autumn 1831, the Owenite Alexander Campbell, himself originally a joiner, formed the Glasgow and West of Scotland Association for the Protection of Labour (with subdivisions for each craft), subsequently termed the General Union of Glasgow, with co-operative production as a main aim. From this, after the *débâcle* of Owenite projects in 1834, survived a Carpenters' Union, of which Hugh Alexander became secretary. Disputes with the Radical journalist Peter Mackenzie earned it commemoration in the files of his *Gazette* (1835). In 1836 it had a dispute with employers who refused to engage union labour, and succumbed after a disastrous eighteen weeks' strike against a winter wage of 18s. (1837-38); its books were burned.

In March 1836 an organisation was formed in Edinburgh with 55 members; a president, vice-president, secretary, and seven 'councillors' were chosen; one shilling entry money, and subscriptions of one penny a month for local and sixpence for national expenses were prescribed. This became a branch of the Friendly Society (or General Union) of Operative House Carpenters and Joiners of Great Britain and Ireland, founded in 1827. Branches were formed in Dundee, Dunfermline, Kirkcaldy, and Leith by travelling propagandists. A minimum wage of 14s. was stipulated; the standard rate in the city was 18s., elsewhere 14s. to 17s. Two hundred and eighteen members in Edinburgh and 196 in other branches were recorded in April 1837. Knowledge of these details is due to the unique circumstance of an early minute book being now preserved in the National Library of Scotland.

The Masons owed their strength to the prevalence of stone in Scottish building. The earliest reference to organisation appears to be in connection with a strike in Edinburgh for higher wages in 1764. The existence of a union in the 1820's is known through the uncomplimentary reminiscences of Hugh Miller, the journalist and geologist, then a journeyman; he deplored that in about 1828 a strike was called against a reduction of wages from 24s. to 15s., 'the first of the great strikes among workmen of which the public have since seen and heard so much'. The union was accused of intimidation by John Wright, a former official who became an Edinburgh Councillor.

The United Operative Masons of Scotland Society was formed in October 1831; after a long strike (November 1833 to February 1834) it secured 'recognition' and survived the *débâcle* of that year. An Edinburgh branch had a funeral society and other 'benefit' activities; it was associated with other unions in a periodical edited by William Biggar, a printer, probably the fortnightly *Trades Examiner*, of which only two issues are known to have appeared (November 1832). The Glasgow branch also attempted a periodical, with essays on politics, science and morals. The union functioned through local lodges; its seat of government (as was common in pre-railway days) was movable and its organisation weak. In 1835 there was a strike in Edinburgh for an increase of wages to 3s. a day in summer; the current weekly rate was 18s., but it was asserted that the annual weekly average came to about 10s. owing to winter short time. In a case arising from this dispute, some members were acquitted of intimidation, and the legality of combination was affirmed by Sheriff Alison (the Tory historian, who, like his brother, the philanthropic Dr. W. P. Alison, had working-class sympathies). In 1849 a Saturday half-holiday was sought.

The bricklayers, though relatively few, were also organised in the 'thirties, when they tried to enforce a rate of 16s. a week. The only other trade in this group of which there is contemporary record is the cabinetmakers. They were an old craft, and the journeymen had shown remarkable strength under the old regime. In Edinburgh, where minutes for 1831 are extant, they published elaborate printed lists of piece-work prices computed by themselves or in consultation with employers, e.g. in 1805 and 1825. Their position deteriorated, however, and in February 1834, Glasgow operatives were on strike, recognition being refused.

Printers were in a favoured position, and their records have been well preserved and their history written by a professional historian, Sarah Gillespie (1953). As she remarks, 'the organisation of the workmen into a "chapel" is a time-honoured custom, apparently as old as the industry'. The first recorded instance in Scotland, however, is that in the Edinburgh firm of Neill, formed in 1785;

its rules survive. In the early nineteenth century, standing committees existed, comprising delegates from various chapels. As already noted, the Court of Session by Interlocutor in 1804 awarded them a 'scale of prices'. A Glasgow Society was instituted in 1817.

A General Typographical Association of Scotland was formed in August 1836, and was absorbed in 1844 by the National Typographical Association, of which it became the Northern District, with its own board; several local branches existed, and others were formed. The organisation collapsed in the depression of 1846-47, but branches survived, and there was a revival in the early 'fifties. An Edinburgh Journeymen Bookbinders' Union Society was formed in 1822; its 'rules' have been preserved, together with a membership card, probably the oldest surviving in Scotland.

Among those stimulated by the revival of the early 'thirties were the bakers, whose organisation was handicapped by the prevalence of small mastership and the 'living in' system. They preserved amicable relations with the Master Court of Incorporations; for instance a branch in Glasgow made a settlement abjuring the strike weapon. In 1837 journeymen bakers throughout Scotland memorialised employers in favour of cash payments instead of partial receipts in kind. Many agreed voluntarily, others under pressure. A general 12-hour day (5 a.m. to 5 p.m.) was also secured. Edinburgh bakers gained a 64½-hour week by a strike in 1846, and commemorated it by striking a medal.

The existence of a Ploughmen's Union is attested only by the intimation of its virtual extinction (June 1834).

The miners had attained legal emancipation only at the end of the eighteenth century, and still for the main part worked under semi-feudal conditions. The Act of 1799 (*c.* 38), which finally abolished serfdom, included clauses subjecting colliers to the wage regulation enactments and to laws prohibiting 'unlawful combinations'. Coal extraction, especially in the Lothians, was commonly carried on under the direct auspices of the landowner, such as the Duke of Buccleuch and the Marquis of Lothian. With the opening up of the western coal measures, short leases were granted to small entrepreneurs, who occasionally combined mining with farming—e.g. the father of the Bairds of Gartsherrie. As already indicated, such unions as existed were usually of the patronised type; e.g. a 'Friendly and Free Labour Society', formed at Govan in 1826, and a 'Young Men's Society', at the Newbattle Colliery of the Marquis of Lothian (1835).

There were, however, attempts at more independent organisation—e.g. a Glasgow and Clydesdale Association of Operative Colliers (1816), which paid officials, administered oaths and held delegate meetings. In 1817, an Ayrshire County Association was formed by a weaver named Fallhouse Wilson, and engaged in an unsuccessful strike. It was still alive in October 1824, when it affirmed rules which charged £5 entry money to newcomers to the trade, gave strike pay of 7s. and widows' benefit of £1, and claimed 1100-1200 members, with William McAllister as secretary. It sought to restrict output and to substitute fortnightly engagements for the yearly bond which survived from serfdom.

A union in Lanarkshire was also active in the 'twenties, and is said to have increased wages from 3s. 6d. to 5s. per day in 1824; there were strikes in 1826, 1828 and 1832. An attempt at a national organisation was made in 1835; this union waged a 17-week strike in the west in 1837, but ill-success led to its collapse. At the same time, a Midlothian union, centred in Dalkeith, with several hundred members, struck for four months for higher wages; it paid 1s. 6d. strike benefit till funds were exhausted, and it survived only as a friendly society.

LOCAL JOINT ACTION

As notable as these intermittent experiments in particular trades was the initiation in the early 'thirties of local joint organisation. It was probably influenced by the grandiose Owenite conceptions, but in practice was chiefly concerned with political aims, and was most active in the agitation which preceded the Great Reform Bill.

Glasgow was already in the forefront in this respect. Here a United Committee of Trades Delegates met weekly at a Trades Hall in Hanover Street. It had several committees in regular session, and was 'entirely composed of working men, many of whom would have done honour to the highest rank in society'. The 'everlasting adjournment to the tavern after business hours' was however later deplored by James Burn, representative of the

Hatters, in his *Autobiography of a Beggar Boy*. The chairman was Daniel Macaulay, a powerloom tenter, 'a small man with a large mind, fluent in speech and quick in debate'; he died young on 7th September 1835.

The Council held demonstrations in favour of Parliamentary Reform, but it was chronically at variance with other factions, such as that represented by Peter Mackenzie of the *Loyal Reformer's Gazette*, which may be regarded as 'petit bourgeois' in composition. It instituted a journal, *The Herald to the Trades' Advocate*, which ran as a weekly from September 1830 to March 1831, with a circulation ranging from 1250 to 4500; this was apparently edited by the Owenite joiner Alexander Campbell. This was duly followed by the *Trades Advocate*, edited by one Warden, a teacher; of this nothing further is known. Campbell also ran on his own account for several issues (December 1833 to June 1834), until stopped by prosecution, an 'unstamped' monthly called the *Tradesman*; he sought to evade the law by charging no fixed price for copies.

The longest lived and most influential of these journalistic ventures was *The Liberator* commenced in November 1832, chiefly under the control of Thomas Atkinson (1801-33), a bookseller and poet active in Radical politics. It was edited, until his premature death at the age of 41 on 19th October 1836, by John Tait (brother-in-law of Daniel Macaulay), whose journalistic ability was widely recognised. He was succeeded by Dr. John Taylor, the Chartist leader, under whose editorship its circulation rivalled that of *The Glasgow Herald*. Its opponents attributed much of its success to the prominence it gave to advertisements of quack remedies; reliance on unorthodox cures was frequently associated with political radicalism. The paper soon succumbed when Taylor transferred his energies to the national sphere (1838).

The contemporary publication of anti-trade union literature for working-class readers is noted by R. K. Webb—e.g. *The Trades Unionist: Illustrations of Social Depravity* (John Reid, Glasgow 1834), a lecture by James Taylor, 'Effects of Combination', to an Edinburgh Association of the Working Classes (1838), and lectures in 1843-44 by James Simpson, the lawyer pioneer of adult education.

After the passing of the Reform Bill there seems to have been a slackening of interest. Regular organisation was revived at a meeting in December 1833, when delegates from 33 trades met and agreed to intervene in the strike in the building trades; a committee of twelve was constituted. In April 1834, a conference of trades was held, at which were present two delegates from London. It was decided to 'correspond and co-operate' with the organisation in the metropolis. In October, the trades presented an address to Lord Durham, then a Radical hero, and entertained him to a dinner, at which Abram Duncan responded to the toast of 'the Working Classes', and proposed the 'Abolition of the taxes on knowledge'. Representatives of the trades joined in protest against the threatened displacement of the Whig administration in the same year, and in September 1835 collaborated with other Radical bodies in welcoming Daniel O'Connell with an address and a 'soirée'.

Again in September 1837 there was a revival, apparently of an *ad hoc* character, when a United Trades Association was formed to assist the cotton spinners in their dispute; the ubiquitous Alexander Campbell was an office-bearer; coopers, hatters engineers and bakers were among the trades represented.

In Edinburgh, it appears from casual references that a body of 'trades delegates' existed, with William Biggar, a printer, as chairman, and one Dow as secretary. They organised a procession in honour of Earl Grey (September 1834), in which representatives of 33 trades participated, including masons, iron-founders, printers, brewers and plasterers. 'Meetings of the working classes' were arranged on occasion—e.g. to petition for pardon of the Dorchester Labourers and against the change of ministry (December 1834), and to oppose a 'National Fast Day' and Parliamentary grants to the Church (June 1835). Like their Glasgow colleagues they demonstrated in favour of O'Connell and were represented at a banquet in his honour (September 1835).

CHARTISM

By the end of the decade, only fragmentary relics of trade unionism survived. Such organisation as existed was largely associated with Chartism. Gatherings of its supporters were commonly described as 'meetings of the working classes', and the local body was sometimes styled 'Workmen's Association'—e.g. in Kilmarnock, Shotts, Tollcross. In Glasgow and Edinburgh, trade sections of adherents were definitely organised, e.g. among Coopers, Masons and Shoemakers in the former, and Coachmakers and Tailors in the latter (1839). 'Delegates from Trades, Shops and Factories' for some time met weekly with the directors of the Glasgow Universal Suffrage Association.

What Cockburn called 'sedition of the stomach' was a recurrent aspect of Chartism, manifest in periods of trade depression and consequent destitution; the connection between the industrial situation and the activity of the movement has been analysed by Dr. L. C. Wright. An outstanding illustration is the Pilgrimage of Folly, a march of strikers from Dundee to Forfar in hopes of stirring up a general strike to enforce the Charter. It was a complete fiasco; John Duncan, a millworker and lay preacher, and other leaders, were imprisoned. In Glasgow, in the 'Forty Eight' there were unemployed demonstrations and riots, which were attributed to Chartist propaganda; demands for amendment of the Poor Law, which precluded relief to the able-bodied, were prominent. 'Parson' Adams, an Owenite, was a leading spokesman.

Many leaders were 'middle class', such as Dr. John Taylor of Ayr, Rev. Patrick Brewster (1788-1859) of Paisley Abbey, the ex-teacher journalist and 'hygeist' John Fraser (1794-1879), who devoted his later life to giving concerts, and the shopkeepers James Moir (1805-80) and George Ross (1790-1858), both of Glasgow, and Hugh Craig (1795-1858) of Kilmarnock. Several artisans were also conspicuous, among them Matthew Cullen, a powerloom weaver, chairman of the Central Chartist Committee, Abram Duncan, a turner, formerly of the Glasgow United Trades, noted as an orator ('the platform is his kingdom'), and William Pattison, secretary of a machinemakers' union. A Committee of Trades Delegates and Directors of the Universal Suffrage Association (1839) had James Proudfoot (d. 1855) as president, Cullen as vice-president and Ross as treasurer. An Edinburgh Tailors' Universal Suffrage Association was formed later that year.

Scottish Chartism maintained not only an independent organisation but distinctive characteristics, derived from national peculiarities and traditions, which link it with the Covenanters and the

'Political Martyrs' of the Revolutionary period. It professed a religious and ethical basis. Chartist Churches were established in Glasgow, Alloa, Arbroath, Dundee, Greenock and elsewhere, and in Glasgow acquired St. Ann's Church (nicknamed the 'Noddy Kirk') which became the 'largest and most popular religious body in the west of Scotland'; services were conducted and sacraments administered by lay preachers such as Charles McEwan and Malcolm McFarlane (d. 1861), later agent of the Scottish Temperance League. Scottish members, with the notable exception of Taylor, tended to support the 'moral force' or constitutionalist position in the recurrent controversy which divided the movement. One of its most lasting contributions to the Scottish working-class movement was its advocacy of total abstinence from alcoholic liquors, a cause rapidly spreading in this period. The Central Committee in 1841 issued an appeal 'to dedicate this year to total abstinence'. A striking illustration lies in the number of coffee-houses and temperance hotels founded by Chartists such as Robert Cranston (1815-92) and John Grant, which became the favourite venues for trade union meetings. Another continuing factor was the support of organised emigration, voiced by, among others, Patrick Matthew, an Angus laird, who promoted settlement in New Zealand; in his volume on arboriculture he later claimed to have anticipated Darwin's theory of natural selection. Alexander Campbell was also involved in Canadian emigration schemes.

There was a widely circulated Chartist press, including the *Liberator*, which did not survive Taylor's departure, the *True Scotsman* (1838-41) of Edinburgh, edited by John Fraser, the *Scottish Patriot* of Robert Malcolm (1781-1850) of Glasgow, and the later *North British Express*, Edinburgh (1846-48). The *Chartist Circular*, the official organ, was rather a magazine than a newspaper.

Scottish Chartism gradually merged in the Radical wing of Gladstonian Liberalism, which dominated the sympathies of trade unionists in the next period. Typical examples are James Moir, associated with the Glasgow Political Union of 1831, who became president of the Scottish National Reform League in 1869, and had long service on Glasgow Town Council; and Robert Cochran (1808-97), son of a 'Reformer of 1793', a handloom weaver who established a drapery business in Paisley in

1850, and became provost of that burgh (1885-88), Allan Pinkerton, who migrated to U.S.A., achieved a very different reputation there as an organiser of a strike-breaking force. Hugh Craig, James Martin and James Adams are said, like Wilkes and Burdett, to have 'died in the odour of Toryism'.

The Owenites, while generally favourable to the Charter, deprecated the importance attached to political reforms; their chief Scottish exponent, Alexander Campbell, was at this time engaged as an itinerant 'missionary' south of the Border.

Small-scale local co-operative societies—e.g. Fenwick Weavers (1769)—existed in the eighteenth century, chiefly to purchase flour and other foodstuffs wholesale and retail them to their members. The Lennoxtown Society, which recently celebrated its 150th anniversary, is the doyen of Scottish societies; one at Govan (1777) survived until 1909. Owen, though the patron saint, is no longer regarded as the founder of the movement; but partly under his influence many societies, mostly short-lived, were founded about 1830. These included 'Bazaars' or labour exchanges, seeking to eliminate a monetary medium, and the Orbiston Community, near Motherwell (1825-27), the sole Scottish example of a self-contained 'communist' settlement. The society at Cambuslang (*c.* 1830) is said to have anticipated, on the advice of Campbell, the expedient of 'dividend on purchase'; his claim to have originated the idea and to have been consulted by the Rochdale Pioneers is regarded as unproven but probably justified.

CHAPTER III

THE MID-CENTURY REVIVAL

As has been indicated, the early trade union movement in Scotland collapsed to a large extent in the course of the 'thirties. During the 'forties, apart from such semi-political societies as were associated with Chartism, organisation seems to have taken the form of local benefit clubs, for such purposes as insurance of tools and provision for funerals.

Meantime a change in the economic structure of the country was becoming manifest. The textiles which had dominated the earlier phase of the industrial revolution were giving place to the heavy industries, especially engineering and shipbuilding, based on the now developed coal and iron mines of the Clyde valley, where the bulk of enterprise had become concentrated. The cotton industry in particular had declined, largely under the pressure of competition from Lancashire; a final blow was dealt by the American Civil War, which cut off supplies. The revival of trade unionism in the 'fifties, as conditions improved after the troubles of the 'forties, reflects the change in the balance of economic power.

The unions of cotton spinners and weavers, while not extinct, became almost negligible. The handloom weavers indeed died hard; as late as 1872 they were reckoned to number about 10,000. In November 1851 at a delegate conference in Glasgow, a union was reformed, as the Manufacturing Weavers' Protection Association for Scotland; the average wage was stated to be 4s. to 4s. 6d.; there were about 1000 unemployed in Paisley, now the main centre. The Government were memorialised to subsidise emigration, and to assimilate the Scottish Poor Law to that of England, so as to legalise relief to the able-bodied. During the next year, weekly delegate meetings were held, seeking to 'suppress nefarious dealing'. More prosperous conditions and increased pay were reported at a conference of Scottish and Irish delegates in April 1853. Improvement was short-lived, and hopes came to rest largely on emigration, as was common at this period. A Central Board of Handloom Weavers' Emigration Association was active in September 1854. A local association was among the first unions to affiliate to Glasgow Trades Council in December 1858. In 1864 a Handloom Weavers' Association existed at Bridgeton (Glasgow), when its secretary, Henry Carrigan, gave evidence to a government committee of the destitution of his fellows. Similar statements were made to the Factory Commission in 1875 by John Mackay, secretary of the Operative Weavers' Society.

Handloom weavers were sometimes congregated under supervision of the employer instead of working in their own homes; hence the proposed formation in 1853 of a union of Factory Handloom Weavers. As the use of steam power increased, the powerloom Weavers were organised; a union in Glasgow struck for higher pay in April 1849, and was met with a threat of a general lockout.

An Association of Amalgamated Weavers of Scotland and Ireland was formed in 1872. Relations between Ulster and West of Scotland textile industries, especially linen, were close; many handworkers had been employed by Glasgow firms.

In 1849 the Glasgow Cotton Spinners Association opposed the introduction of the 'relay' system, designed to circumvent legal restriction of working hours. In the later 'sixties it subsidised emigration.

The Operative Bleachers conducted a 'short time' agitation about 1860 with the aid of Glasgow Trades Council, and demanded extension of the Factory Acts. The Block Printers' Trade Union of Paisley and Barrhead, influenced by the Christian Socialist Rev. Thomas G. Lee, sponsored a co-operative factory in November 1851.

Hawick Hosiery Framework Knitters had no increase from 1835 to 1871, when the rent of 1s. for the frame was abolished. In November 1872 they struck against the continuance of other deductions, amounting to about 3s., from a wage of 19s. to 21s. They received a grant in aid from the Joiners.

There were a few small and exclusive unions of men engaged in specialised processes in textile factories, which were predominantly staffed by female labour.

Yarn Dyers were involved in an unsuccessful dispute in Glasgow in 1869. A Glasgow branch of the Nine Hour Factory Act Association existed in 1874.

After a disastrous strike of about 3000 operatives for seven weeks, when a 5 per cent cut was accepted, the East of Scotland Factory Workers' Association was formed in Dundee in 1875; in spite of its 3000 members, it seems to have been short-lived.

THE MINERS

It was in coal-mining that the most important advance in trade unionism was made during this period. The industry was still largely in the hands of the landowner, or of short-term and small-scale lessees—individuals or co-partneries. It was only after the legalisation of limited liability in 1862 that the joint stock company became at all common in extractive and constructional industries; e.g. the Arniston, Benhar and Clyde Coal Companies in the 'seventies.

It was while these changes in capitalist structure were commencing that the first real national union of miners was accomplished; the story is fully told in R. Page Arnot's *History*. Earlier efforts in 1835-37 and 1844-47 had left little trace, though in 1849 Tremenheere, the Mines Commissioner, reported that there was considerable combination in the west to restrict labour, which, he held, resulted in lower wages than were obtained by the unorganised employees of large firms such as Bairds, Wilsons, and Addie and Miller.

The new achievement was mainly the work of one man, Alexander Macdonald. Born in 1821, the son of a Lanarkshire miner, he worked in the pits from the age of eight. At 21 he utilised his savings to study at Glasgow University. For a few years he conducted a private school in his native district, giving his spare time to trade union agitation. Having somehow acquired 'a modest fortune by a series of successful commercial speculations', from about 1852 he devoted himself entirely to organising his former fellow-workers. Out of a series of conferences emerged in 1855 the United Coal and Iron Miners' Association of Scotland 'for the protection of miners' rights and privileges, by providing funds for the support of members out of work'. It was a federation of local societies, with a central executive of three, and Macdonald as secretary. The entry fee was sixpence, and weekly subscription one penny. The programme included arbitration in trade disputes, the encouragement of apprenticeship, compulsory education, and the appointment of checkweighmen. The last-mentioned demand was accorded by an Act of 1860. The first president of the Association was Dan McLaughlin, of Denny in Stirlingshire. The calling of a general strike against 'the Masters' Special Rules' was approved in the spring of 1856 by a majority of two to one, but Macdonald's influence was exercised for negotiation.

He also opposed the policy of the 'restricted darg' (output), frequently pursued in the hope of raising prices by scarcity value. A shorter hours movement was afoot in the late 'sixties, when an attempt was made to introduce blacklegs from Cornwall into Lanarkshire. Union policy was first concentrated on reforms in the 'offtake' system and the abolition of truck. 'Offtakes' were deductions made from wages for tools and lighting, and also for medical and educational services; these were common in collieries, and were resented, especially as administration by employers of the fund thus raised was sometimes suspect. The prohibition of truck by an Act of 1831 was chronically evaded by various devices in many Scottish mines and ironworks, whose remoteness had, in the absence of ordinary shopping facilities, given some pretext for the continuance of company stores. Other grievances included bad ventilation and inadequate inspection of pits; it was complained in 1856 that there were only two inspectors for 1640 pits. The arrestment of wages for debt was another long-standing injury to workers generally; Macdonald was active in an agitation which eventuated in an amendment of the law, which exempted from liability 'alimentary' wages up to 20s. (1870).

Macdonald extended his activities beyond the Border, and at a conference in Leeds in November 1863 a National Union of Miners, 36,000 strong, was founded, whose presidency he held till his death. This was a loose federation. Macdonald received no salary, but a maintenance allowance and refund of expenses when engaged on union business. The Scottish connection with this body was rather intermittent. In 1870, no Scottish members were recorded, but in 1873 delegates claimed to represent 18,000 members, and John Gillespie of Falkirk was appointed secretary, an honorary post.

Despairing of the strike weapon, Macdonald pursued two lines of action. Reverting to the old idea of co-operative production, he encouraged the acquisition of collieries by miners, but without success; and he promoted a Scottish Miners' Emigration Association (1865) to defray the passages to America of unemployed miners, and thus relieve the labour market; he thrice visited the United States to investigate mining conditions there. He also employed the method of legal enactment. He sought the relief of employees from criminal liability for breach of contract of service; this was partly accorded by the Master and Servant Act of 1867 and completely by the Employers and Workmen Act of 1875.

Macdonald obtained the 'Miners' Charter' in the comprehensive Act of 1872. Legal limitation of working hours, and workmen's compensation for industrial injuries were sought in vain. Macdonald won the miners to the idea of trade union representation in Parliament; having stood down in Kilmarnock Burghs in 1868, he secured Liberal endorsement as a candidate for the two-seated constituency of Stafford in 1874, and held the seat for the rest of his life; his electoral expenses were partly paid by the Scottish miners.

Macdonald became first chairman of the Parliamentary Committee of the Trades Union Congress on its inception in 1871. In 1874, on his own responsibility, he accepted membership of the Government Commission on Trade Union law, and presented a minority report. His independent attitude in this instance, his recommendation to accept wage reductions of 20 per cent in 1874, and his repudiation of unauthorised strikes during the depression, evoked considerable criticism, voiced notably by Daniel Brown, a Glasgow accountant. But Macdonald, who was indefatigable in propaganda throughout the country, seems to have retained the confidence of the majority till the last; he died in October 1881.

Scottish delegate conferences were held periodically during the 'sixties and 'seventies, and in 1866 an attempt was made to strengthen national organisation by the formation of a Coal and Ironstone Miners' Mutual Protection Association of Scotland. The constitution provided for weekly allowances in cases of strike, lockout or injury, death benefits, a subscription of 6d. per week for members between 17 and 50, 3d. for those from 12 to 17. The ordinary subscription comprised labour dues 3d., accident and death 2d., executive 1d. The Association was to be administered by an executive and district committees.

John Gillespie of Falkirk acted latterly as chairman of the Scottish Union, re-organised on a federal basis in October 1873. James Keir Hardie was appointed secretary in October 1879. By this date, however, all national organisation was virtually defunct, though the Association was not formally dissolved until November 1882.

The real strength and vitality of mining unionism lay in the local associations; some of these however had a sporadic existence. Free Colliers' Lodges or friendly societies of a quasi-masonic character existed, especially in the west, in the middle 'sixties; a Miners' Free Brotherhood of Scotland, with James Simpson as Master, was at least formally constituted in 1865. These were encouraged to give 'greater permanency to the Union' by offering disablement and death benefits; they held annual excursions and other social functions.

A Midlothian County Union was formed in 1853, and advocated time rates of payment. In 1863 a Labour Protection and Sick Benefit Society was formed there, with John Nicholson of Niddrie as Grand Master; this was soon dissolved. A Mid and East Lothian Miners' Association was formed in December 1871, and by 1873 had 2000 members and funds of £1200; Thomas Wilson of Bonnyrigg was a leading figure and David Moffat (grandfather of Abe) secretary till, being victimised, he removed to Fife. Shale miners in the rising mineral oil industry were temporarily organised in a Shale Miners' Protection Society, in the Calders area at least. The County Association was still active in 1877, when an entry fee of 1s. 6d. was charged, and conferences were held with employers. Two years later, membership had fallen to 250, and dissolution of the society and division of its funds of some £2500 was voted by a large majority. This however was interdicted, and the union was reconstituted, under the leadership of Wilson and Alexander Cook of Arniston. It was, however, again almost extinct in the early 'eighties.

The most enduring and efficient organisation was that of the Fife and Kinross Miners, which has existed without a break since 1869. It was the first to obtain recognition from the employers, and gained the 8-hour day by agreement in 1870. Its entry fee was half a crown, and weekly subscription 3d.; it paid 16s. a week accident or victimisation benefit. It was associated with the national body, but often took an independent line. It owed much to the able leadership of Richard Penman, its first president, who died in March 1873, and Henry Cook of Lochgelly, secretary from the start till his death in July 1880, when he was succeeded by John Weir. It successfully survived a lockout in 1877.

Stirlingshire had a union dating from 1871, with which West Lothian was intermittently associated; in 1874 it claimed over 3000 members, with Alexander Abercromby as president and William Holms as secretary. Its outstanding figure was John Gillespie of Falkirk, also prominent in the national union. As national organiser he appealed for help from Glasgow Trades Council (June 1874).

In Lanarkshire and Ayrshire several small unions rose and fell. Regular meetings at Holytown are reported in 1852-53. Associations at Wishaw (formed 1869), Maryhill and Larkhall were represented at the conference of 1873, with a total membership of about 3500. Larkhall seems to have been the steadiest area; its organisation was reconstructed in 1874 as the Larkhall Miners' Mutual Protection Accident and Funeral Association. Its delegate, Hector McNeil, took an active part in national affairs, and Robert Smillie first appeared as its secretary. A Lanarkshire union was in being in 1874, with J. Muir as chairman and T. Smith secretary; in 1879 Keir Hardie was appointed agent. A popular method of action in this district was 'putting on the block'—i.e. balloting as to which colliery should go on strike; those on whom the lot fell were maintained by their fellows who remained at work in the other pits. In the late summer of 1879 took place a famous 'tattie' (potato) strike, over which Hardie came into conflict with the veteran Macdonald. This resulted in the collapse of trade unionism in the western mines for some years. An Ayrshire union is mentioned in 1853; it was re-formed in 1866, but broke up in August 1881; Hardie was secretary during its last year.

In the early 'eighties there was thus a period of general stagnation, partly the outcome of the trade depression, which peculiarly affected the heavy industries and also reacted on others.

BUILDING TRADES

The building trades also had a period of prosperity during the 'Years of Plenty', and survived the era of depression, though with diminished strength. The Scottish United Operative Masons had little more than a nominal existence during the 'forties; in 1848 they struck in Glasgow for 12½ per cent advance on a wage then averaging £1. The Glasgow branch is also credited with a pioneer venture in workers' education, in the formation during this decade of 'a class for mutual instruction and an association for moral physical and intellectual improvement'.

About 1850 the national union was reorganised with assistance from England; it grew rapidly within the next few years, and appointed a full-time secretary in 1855, when it had 31 Lodges and some 3000 members. Its headquarters were in Glasgow; 'idle benefit' amounted to 6s. a week, and an 'emigration bonus' of £3 was awarded to departing members. A feature of administration was the appointment of 'collectors' or shop stewards, and they maintained 'Houses of Call'. Continuing the educational tradition, the Nelson Street chapel in Glasgow established in 1857 an Artisans' Drawing Club. The union sought reduction of the working day and payment by the hour in substitution for the usual fortnightly reckoning. 'Nine Hour Committees' were formed throughout Scotland from 1859 to 1861; after a three months' struggle (March to June 1861), they achieved that object in Edinburgh, and it was virtually universal in Scotland by 1866.

This movement was 'distinctly the starting-point of a new phase of the labour question'. Out of the Edinburgh dispute also emerged a Co-operative Building Society which attained much greater success than most such productive ventures, but gradually lost its co-operative character and trade union connections. Some rows of two-storey dwellings erected by it can still be seen in Edinburgh at Abbeyhill, Canonmills and elsewhere. A similar society in Glasgow commenced operations at Farme (Rutherglen) in 1874.

Membership of the Union rose to 11,000 by 1875, and nearly 14,000 in over 80 lodges in 1877, with reserve funds of £18,000. This was mainly due to the exceptionally able administration of Matthew Allan, secretary from 1867 to 1883; headquarters were then in Greenock, where Allan and a central committee of twelve all resided. In September 1878, the failure of the City of Glasgow Bank, where the bulk of its funds were deposited, crippled its activities. The disaster also intensified depression in the building trades; consequently by 1883 membership had fallen to under 6000, and capital to £1800.

A Protective Association of Joiners of Glasgow and the West of Scotland existed prior to 1847, when it possessed a mutual insurance fund for tools; 115 members were then insured for from £5 to £15, paying premiums of threepence in the pound. In 1861 it was dissolved, and the balance shared among 34 members. A United Joiners and House Carpenters of the City of Glasgow Society was formed in September 1849. Its 38 rules included 'amicable adjustment of matters in dispute' by arbitration. As the subscription was one penny a week, the only benefit was 10s. a week for strike or lockout. Legal proceedings involving the principles of the Society were borne by it. A collector was appointed for each shop or squad.

In September 1861 this local body was absorbed in an Associated Carpenters' and Joiners' Society formed at a delegate meeting in Edinburgh where, after a strike, it evolved from a society for the insurance of tools. The society started with eleven lodges and 630 members; it soon extended its scope to England. Besides providing various mutual benefits, it avowedly stood for the maintenance and advancement of trade interests. Benefits continued to include insurance of tools; levies were 3d. a week for the trade section and 3d. for the benefit section, which was optional, but included two-thirds of the membership. There was at first a movable executive, fluctuating between the two large branches, Edinburgh and Glasgow, with a spare-time secretary. George Ross, the first secretary, became in 1865 secretary of the Associated Carpenters and Joiners of Scotland Building Society, a joint stock company of which all shareholders were members of the trade union.

Despite the loss of its records, the course of the society can be followed, thanks to frequent reports in the contemporary press and to the evidence collected by Mr. S. Higenbotham in his *History of the Amalgamated Society of Woodworkers*, its present successor. Hours were 51 to 60 per week, wages from 17s. to 24s. Considerable advance was made under the secretaryship (1867-83) of William Paterson (1843-1906), afterwards the first workman Factory Inspector in Scotland and Firemaster of Glasgow. It showed considerable militancy and gained increased wages and reduced hours; piecework was rejected as 'violating a vital principle of the Society'. It survived the slump with some loss of membership and resources, dropping nearly half of its total of about 9000 members between 1878 and 1880; hours of labour in the shipyards were again increased from 51 to 54.

This Associated Society contended with the rivalry of the Amalgamated Society of Carpenters and Joiners formed in 1860 in London by Robert Applegarth, on a basis of high contributions and benefits, and opposition to strikes; it established several Scottish branches from 1870, and at its peak claimed 5000 members, but lost many in the early 'eighties. The 'Associated' negotiated reciprocity with this and other English unions in 1865, but formed English and Irish branches in 1874, and dropped 'Scottish' from its title in 1887.

The other building trades were less active and influential. The United Operative Slaters of Glasgow affiliated to the United Trades Committee in 1853. In May 1866 the Amalgamated Slaters' Society of Scotland was formed at a delegate conference in Glasgow; it remained for some time small and ineffective, but weathered the storm of the late 'seventies best of the building trades, since its members were chiefly engaged in jobbing and repairing; they preserved their standard rate of 6½d. per hour. It provided strike and funeral benefits for a contribution of 4d. a week.

The United Operative Plumbers Association was reconstituted in 1865 as a national body, with Edinburgh and Glasgow branches; it enforced apprenticeship and forbade piecework. In 1872 a breakaway occurred in Glasgow on the ground that 'more money went out of Scotland than came into it'. Centralisation in Liverpool had for some years occasioned friction. The United Operative Plumbers of Scotland thus came into being in July 1872, and kept an independent life, though with only a handful of members; the majority of the Scottish lodges adhered to the parent body.

The United Operative Plasterers' Benefit and Protection Society existed before June 1869, when its rules were amended; it established a remarkably high position, with a minimum hourly rate of 10d., and rigid control of apprenticeship, but it was ruined by a lengthy strike following the building collapse of 1878, and unionism became almost extinct for a decade.

In 1853 a Scottish Painters' Society was formed in Glasgow; it seems to have absorbed an earlier Glasgow Operative Painters'

Society, and an Edinburgh branch is mentioned in 1856. It induced the employers to settle disputes in an arbitration court. It adopted a 9-hour policy, and claimed 2500 members. It was reorganised in 1859. A lockout followed, the employers alleging a breach of agreement; an animated controversy was carried on in the press and several firms supported the cause of the union. A National House and Ship Painters' Association, centred in Glasgow, adopted a 9-hour policy, and claimed 2500 members (1866); a Mutual Protection Society is also referred to about this date. Organisation, however, remained virtually local till the late 'eighties. A successful strike for increased rates was waged in 1874. A strike in Edinburgh in 1877 was supported by the General Alliance of Painters in England, Scotland and Ireland, presumably the so-called Manchester Alliance.

A Glasgow Bricklayers Operative Society was founded in 1850, and its rules revised in 1858; its members had an average wage of 7½d. an hour, with 50 per cent extra for overtime and double pay for Sunday work; return fares were paid for travelling to jobs in the country. It sought restriction of apprentices and rejected piecework; in 1867 it obtained a 55-hour week and a daily wage of 5s. 6d.; William C. Hamilton was secretary. An Operative Bricklayers' Association of Scotland existed in 1875, with 7000 members.

HEAVY INDUSTRIES

We now turn to the shipbuilding and engineering trades on which the prosperity of Scotland, and especially of the Clyde, was coming to be peculiarly and rather precariously based. Here a considerable solidarity among employers is noticeable; the Clyde Shipbuilders and Engineers Association was formed in 1866; it displayed an anti-union attitude.

The woodworkers' unions generally sought to organise shipyard as well as housebuilding employees. Shipwrights appear to have been organised on the Clyde by 1840, and are said to have maintained a 'closed shop' policy for about sixteen years prior to a strike in 1856 in Dumbarton and another in 1857 in Glasgow. These were broken through importation of blacklegs by such prominent firms as Denny and Napier; for some years thereafter a pledge of non-unionism, described as 'signing the line', was exacted, and seven-years apprenticeship accepted. A Glasgow Shipwrights' Society is, however, recorded in 1858, and joined in forming the Associated Shipwrights' Society in 1863. It was primarily provident and its funds were exhausted by a lockout of the shipbuilding trades of the Clyde from May to August 1866, settled by negotiation with the Clyde Shipbuilders' Association. Wages previously had averaged 36s.; they now fell by 10s., and within the next twenty years touched their former height only once and that for a short time. In the early 'eighties, the union had about 3000 members in the Glasgow area, all skilled, with five-years apprenticeship. They were chiefly paid time rates, and hours had fallen from 60 to 54, for some years even to 51.

The Associated Blacksmiths (sometimes called Hammermen) or Operative Blacksmiths' Protective and Friendly Society was formed in August 1857 as an outcome of a strike in Greenock for the 51-hour week. By 1865 it numbered 1700 members in 27 branches. Its rules were revised in 1866 and 1872. In 1875 it had some 2000 members, but declined somewhat. It was associated with the Iron Trades Shorter Hours Committee established, under the chairmanship of Robert Rankin, an engineer, in 1866, and with a later 51-hour movement on the Clyde and East Coast in 1872. The Dundee branch was dissolved on attaining its demand in August 1872. John Inglis (1834-1910) was secretary of the Blacksmiths for nearly half a century (1863-1910), and became prominent in the Trades Union Congress.

The Amalgamated Society of Engineers (A.S.E.), the first great 'model union', absorbed in 1851 seven branches of the Scottish Steam Enginemakers, which had existed in the late 'thirties when William Pattison the Chartist was secretary, and had then possessed a hall; it had been reconstructed in 1849. Glasgow, Greenock, Edinburgh and Kirkcaldy unanimously favoured amalgamation; Dundee and Aberdeen showed considerable majorities against. There was recurrent friction regarding local autonomy. In 1867 there were over 3000 Scottish members in fully thirty branches. Hours of labour had been reduced to 57 or less when in the spring of 1871 a struggle for the 51-hour week was launched at a conference in Glasgow of interested trades; a Clyde Short Time League, of which Thomas R. Elrick, an engineer, was secretary, negotiated with the Master Shipbuilders.

The demand was conceded in Glasgow, to commence in November 1872, but the railway shops, notorious for long hours, soon forced an extension to 54, and this example was followed generally as the depression became acute. Hence the existence about 1880 of a 51 Hours Recovery League in Glasgow, and a Defence Association in Edinburgh.

A Journeymen Machine Engine and Iron Grinders' Friendly Society, established in Glasgow in 1846, still existed at the end of the century; its entry fee was £2, and dues a shilling a week.

The A.S.E. gave Scotland the first example not merely of a highly organised union but of one with an efficient central control outwith Scottish soil. Another such was the United Society of Boilermakers and Iron Shipbuilders, formed in 1832, which had a very strong and undivided organisation throughout the country. A Boilermakers' Friendly Society is mentioned in Glasgow in May 1840; its connection with the national body is uncertain, but by 1856 the latter had branches on the Clyde; during a lockout in Dumbarton in that year, 11s. strike benefit was paid. The Boilermakers gave a precedent for a 'Triple Alliance' by co-operating with the A.S.E. and the Ironfounders in setting up a reserve fund for use against employers. This was followed by a lockout (May to October 1877) which ended in a stalemate. The Boilermakers lost £30,000, but stayed out till February 1879; this sectional action left hostility between them and the A.S.E. The rules of the society stipulated three-years apprenticeship and a proportion of one apprentice to five journeymen.

An Associated Patternmakers' Society had a brief existence in Glasgow in the 'seventies. The United Kingdom Patternmakers' Association, formed in 1872, established branches in Dundee (1874) and in Glasgow (1877); there was friction with the A.S.E. The Associated Bolt and Nut Makers of Scotland were formed in November 1855 and reorganised in March 1873.

The Associated Society of Ironmoulders of Scotland dated from 1831, and was thus the doyen of the iron trade; its members were reckoned as skilled workers. The Glasgow branch was in 1838 the 'seat of government'; its secretary acted as general secretary. McGowan was the first regular secretary, 1845-50, and was succeeded by William Lees (1850-52) and David Adamson, an Owenite (1852-60). Mutual Improvement Classes and a library were formed, emigration grants were given, and action

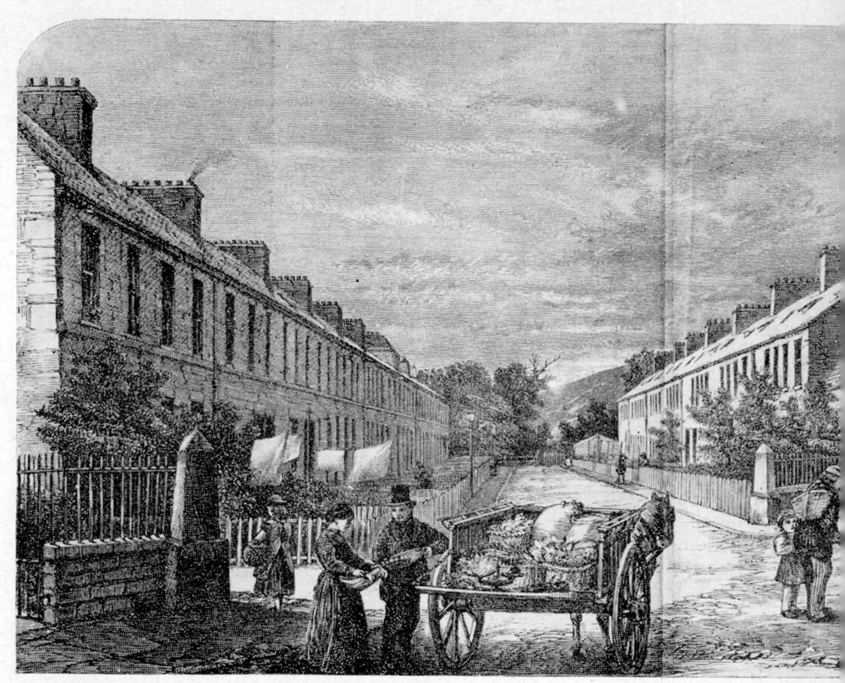

National Library of Scotland

Hugh Miller Place (looking North)

WORKMEN'S CO-OPERATIVE DWELLINGS

Reid Terrace and Hugh Miller Place, Edinburgh

Examples of co-operative building in 1860's

(page 29)

C. S. Minto, Edinburgh City Librarian

taken against speeding up and respiratory diseases. The Union sought consistently to assert restriction of apprenticeship, on which issue it exhausted funds of £11,000 in an unsuccessful strike (1846-47). These restrictions were subsequently enforced until the employers combined to lock them out during a slump in 1868, and after a nine weeks' struggle compelled a surrender of their privileges. The Union survived and was able a few years later to advance wages and obtain the 51-hour week (1872), but its funds were drained in the subsequent slump, and it had to reduce benefit. Its membership had risen from about 3000 in the mid 'sixties to over 5000 in the 'seventies. Colin Steele, a working moulder for twenty years, was secretary 1860-66, succeeded by Robert Skimming (1866-69) and John Fraser (1870-79). A rival Operative Ironmoulders' Friendly Society, formed in April 1869, was absorbed in 1875. It had regular negotiations with the Scottish Ironfounders Association from about 1863.

Two small unions were the Scottish Iron Dressers, with under 200 members in 1856, and the Scottish Operative Brass-founders (1856). An Edinburgh Sheet Metal Workers' Union of about 1870 is commemorated in banners which it displayed in Labour Law Reform demonstrations.

Employees in the ironworks proper were first organised by the Associated Society of Iron and Steel Workers, formed in 1862, with headquarters at Darlington, under the direction of John Kane (d. 1876); it adhered to the sliding-scale principle. A Union of Iron Puddlers at Coatbridge is mentioned in 1864, but after a dispute in the mid 'sixties, when arbitration was refused by the employers, non-unionism seems to have prevailed in Scotland for two decades. The relation of the so-called National Association of Puddlers, of whose west of Scotland branch John Matthews, who retired in 1865, was first secretary, to the Associated Society is obscure. A strike in the malleable iron trade in Coatbridge in January 1871 is reported to have been organised by Kane.

The railwaymen had friendly societies dating from the 'fifties—e.g. the Caledonian and the Glasgow and South Western employees; a Locomotive Engine Drivers and Firemen's Amalgamated Benefit Society secured concessions from the Scottish companies about 1867. The first permanent trade union was the Amalgamated Society of Railway Servants, founded in 1871, which for twenty years remained under philanthropic patronage;

it opened branches in Edinburgh and Glasgow in 1876. A separate society was inaugurated in March 1872; George Weston, a North British engine-driver, was appointed chairman, with an executive of twelve, and Robert Gordon, followed by Joseph Hope, as secretary. The objects were stated as: 'to promote a good and fair understanding between employers and employed', to prevent strikes, secure an increase of pay and reduction of hours, extra pay for overtime, and defence of members prosecuted. Intoxication on duty was to involve a fine and suspension from benefit. This union formed about 20 branches within a few years, and acquired a membership of about 2000. Relations with the English union varied; there was opposition to the formation of its branches in Scotland and persistent disagreement between their delegates at Edinburgh Trades Council; but negotiations recurred, and both societies co-operated in 1881 in a Nine Hours Movement Committee for Railway Servants.

CONSUMPTIONAL TRADES

Among the consumptional trades, still usually small-scale concerns, printers, tailors and bakers were best organised, and each contributed notable personalities to Scottish trade unionism. The Scottish Typographical Society, re-established independently in 1853, conducted negotiations through a central Board. Female labour is said to have been first introduced in a local strike in 1872, and remained a chronic grievance. The society was, however, able to maintain apprenticeship rules and improve wage and hour conditions. 'Honest John' Battersby (1839-1922), its Glasgow secretary from 1873 to 1886, was prominent in the Trades Council and latterly a veteran of municipal politics. A Monthly Circular was issued. In 1867 piece rates were reported general; individual advances on minima were frequently granted.

Rudiments of trade unionism, as already noted, existed among journeymen tailors in the late eighteenth century, and a Glasgow union is mentioned in 1822, but permanent organisation cannot be traced earlier than about 1850. Although the technique of the trade altered little, and processes remained 'domestic', the multiple shop, dealing in ready-made garments, was appearing; Hyams of Leeds were pioneers in Scotland in the 'sixties. A

Journeymen Tailors' Union operated in Glasgow from 1850, and joined in forming a Federal Union of Scotland, which held its first national conference in August 1851; a Western Executive Council and Edinburgh and Aberdeen District Councils were formed. In Glasgow, perhaps under the influence of Kingsley, a Tailors' Co-operative Society was also formed (November 1850). An Edinburgh union, which seems to have stood apart, accepted amalgamation in December 1865. A national dispute took place in the spring of 1866 and resulted in the grant of advanced wage rates, the 'London Log' being taken as a basis. A subsequent attempt of employers to undercut, by importing labour from Denmark and Germany, was frustrated. Scottish employers joined a newly formed Master Tailors Association of the United Kingdom; but the journeymen, who had branches in 32 towns and levied 6d. per head per annum for national purposes, declined to amalgamate with the English union and were on rather unfriendly terms for many years. Glasgow was retained as the seat of the executive. Membership rose to 4500 in 84 branches. The union took an active part in the political reform agitation of the 'sixties, when John Stewart was president and William Cobb secretary; that post was held in 1875 by Henry Wright. Such members as William Troup, John McWhinnie and Neil McLean were dominant figures in Edinburgh Trades Council during this period.

An Operative Bakers' National Association of Scotland was established in 1846. At its strongest, in the 'fifties, when John Bennett was secretary, it had about 3000 members, paying 2d. per week, and had secured 'dry pay', i.e. a cash wage. From the 'sixties, it suffered through displacement of men by machinery. In 1865 a presentation was made to Charles Lang, secretary and ex-president. An Edinburgh Operative Bakers' Provident Society was formed as an off-shoot about 1875. The Association was disrupted by a disastrous strike in 1877, the regular 10-hour day being lost, and the membership falling to 2000. Local societies persisted in the chief centres, and struggled against such grievances as a very early morning start—sometimes 3 a.m. (as commemorated by Harry Lauder)—and ill-lit and insanitary bakehouses. Apprenticeship was nominally five years, but was not generally enforced after the introduction of machinery. Employers were as a rule small men, and strongly anti-unionist.

The outstanding representative of the workers was Archibald Jeffrey Hunter (1820-1903), secretary of the Glasgow branch, for whom he secured a Saturday half-holiday; he was afterwards secretary of Glasgow Trades Council, and an early Labour town councillor.

The 'fifties and 'sixties witnessed the formation of unions in miscellaneous trades, usually ephemeral. Glasgow Boot and Shoe Operatives had a Protective Society which waged a strike in the spring of 1853. The Edinburgh Society retained the old-fashioned designation of Cordwainers. A strike in Edinburgh and other centres in 1866 resulted in a compromise; a Joint Committee was formed to grade wages in five 'classes'. Delegates from 36 Scottish centres a few months later united in a National Society whose programme included a 60-hour week and a minimum rate of 4d. per hour. Within a year there were some 70 branches and 2000 members. Edinburgh served as 'seat of government' under a general secretary named Jackson.

Representatives from Aberdeen and Glasgow attended a delegate meeting of Carpetworkers in Yorkshire, and demanded a 10-hour day and 10 per cent increase in wages (1866). In December 1874, powerloom Carpet Weavers of Scotland are mentioned as involved in a dispute with employers.

A National Association of Rope and Twine Spinners of Great Britain had a branch in Glasgow in 1858, and in 1866 supported a strike of ropemakers there against the withdrawal of an advance in wages granted the previous year.

Unionism among Cabinetmakers was flourishing at this date; £3500 was paid in insurance of members' tools, shop organisation was arranged, and wages had risen on the average 7½ per cent.

Among other miscellaneous unions active in the mid-century, to which casual reference has been found, are the United Flint Glass Makers' Friendly Society of Great Britain and Ireland, dating from 1849, which had a branch in Glasgow by 1853—its 'seat of government' 1863-67; and whose general secretary in 1866 was Benjamin Smart of that city; the Federal Society of Nailmakers of the United Kingdom and Ireland, founded 1853, which had a branch at Camelon (Falkirk), a centre of the industry; the United Coopers of Glasgow, who celebrated their thirteenth anniversary in March 1865; the Potters' National Association (*c.* 1860)—with branches in the north of England—whose chairman was George Newton, prominent in the Trades Council; the Operative Bottlemakers' Society, formed in April 1865; the 'Saddlers', who in both Edinburgh and Glasgow gained a 10 per cent wage increase in 1866; and the Glasgow Carters' Association, which claimed about 2000 members in December 1866.

Attempts to organise farm servants began as early as 1805; local unions existed in central Scotland in 1834 and 1845; as in England, larger scale ventures emerged in the 1860's and '70's, notably in Aberdeenshire; local bodies were linked with a Scottish Farm Servants' Protection Association, originating in Midlothian about 1866. Organisation apparently broke down in the early 'seventies.

JOINT ACTION

Perhaps the most important feature of this period was the development of local and national joint action. As previously shown, a delegate council of trades had operated in Glasgow in the 'thirties, and there are traces of something similar in Edinburgh. Whether there was any real continuity between them and the permanent Trades Councils now existing remains uncertain from lack of evidence. Many Glasgow records were lost in a fire at the Albion Hall in 1909, though some believed lost have recently come to light. Edinburgh possesses almost complete minutes from 1859. From these it appears that a regular organisation of Trades Delegates existed continuously from 1849. It was associated with a movement in the 'fifties to secure a general Saturday half-holiday, to further which aim it organised a demonstration in 1853.

When its records commence, the Edinburgh Council includes representatives of 17 trades, such as the Blacksmiths, Brassfounders, French Polishers, Joiners, Masons and Tailors; notably, in the main, small non-factory groups. William Troup of the last-mentioned was president from 1859 to 1866. Meetings were at first held fortnightly in Burden's Coffee House; later, at Buchanan's Temperance Hotel (1866-86). A conspicuous activity was the running of an annual excursion. Public demonstrations were arranged—e.g. to protest against the anti-trade union utterances of Adam Black the publisher, M.P. for the city; and to support the Nine Hours campaign. The Council discussed legislation affecting trade unionism, and sometimes acted in concert with the corresponding body in Glasgow.

In April 1860 the name was changed to the Council of United Trade Delegates, and new rules were adopted. Delegates were sent to the Social Service Association Congresses in Scotland in 1860 and 1863; invitations were accepted to submit to the latter a paper on shorter hours, and also to be guests at a 'supper of Monte Video beef, to test its qualities'; the acceptance observed that 'if it suits their palate they will do ample justice to it'. In 1861 a course of public lectures was arranged; those participating included three university professors. The Council possessed a small lending library; the exchange of books among members was a regular feature. It subscribed to the *Glasgow Sentinel*, because of its 'able advocacy of the rights of the working classes'. It sponsored abortive projects for the establishment of a periodical of its own, *The Scottish Workman and Social Reformer*, and for the acquisition of a Trades Hall. In January 1865 it held a 'meeting of the working classes' to demand amendment of the Master and Servant Act; Troup presided, and Newton and others addressed it.

In 1866 it frequently failed to find a quorum, only three trades being regularly represented. In July 1867 it was reconstituted as the Trades Council of Edinburgh. It adopted a statement defining its purpose as 'the advancement and protection of the rights of labour as also the wellbeing of the working classes generally', and specified seven methods of achieving it, e.g. 'assisting to organise trade societies; petitioning Parliament, and watching over proceedings in the Courts'. This programme it sought to fulfil by sending deputations and questionnaires to M.P.s regarding the trade union legislation then pending. With two dissentients, it approved Free Trade, and it memorialised the Town Council to enforce the Factory Acts. It took a persistent interest in such local concerns as the administration of the Royal Infirmary; after the extension of the franchise it resolved to take part in municipal elections, but complicated negotiations with other factions were inconclusive; in 1879 it unsuccessfully ran candidates for the School Board. It frequently received deputations from trade unionists on strike, and commended their cause to the more active help of affiliated bodies.

In 1875, two standing committees, on local and on Parliamentary affairs, were appointed. Office-bearers were frequently changed; among the leading figures at this period, in addition to those already mentioned, were three blacksmiths, Alexander Dewar, John C. Burn and Alexander Fraser; Cornelius Yorston, secretary 1875-80, and John G. Holburn (1843-99), afterwards a 'Lib-Lab' M.P. In 1869 it appointed the past and present Lord Advocates, Gordon (Tory) and Moncrieff (Liberal) as honorary presidents.

In Glasgow, occasional references occur to meetings of Trades Delegates in the early 'fifties, e.g. in February 1851 regarding representation at a Chartist convention, and from 1853 in support of strikes. In October, a Committee of Trades Delegates was appointed to deal with disputes; it seems to have been dissolved in 1856. In June 1856, a United Trades Committee, representing over twenty trades, with W. B. Campbell as secretary, issued an address in support of the miners, and called a delegate conference, attended by about sixty, some from Aberdeen and Dundee, held in Garrick's Temperance Coffee House, a typical rendezvous.

The formation, or revival, of a regular Council is officially assigned to a meeting held on 13th May 1858; the jubilee was celebrated in 1908, when a brief account was issued; the centenary in 1958 produced a more elaborate brochure. Eight trades were represented—Bakers, Carters, Cotton Spinners, Iron Moulders, Irondressers, Outdoor Labourers, Sawyers, Shoemakers. Meetings were held weekly, and the title 'Council of the United Trades of Glasgow' was soon adopted. The new body concerned itself with demands for the 8-hour day and the relief of unemployment. It further assisted emigration schemes, and endorsed a proposal for interest-free loans for public works, promoted by the veteran Alexander Campbell, now on the staff of the *Sentinel.* He had been actively associated with the formation of the Council, but being no longer an operative was declared ineligible for membership, though allowed to attend in an honorary capacity and to report proceedings.

By 1863, 33 trades were affiliated, representing 6000 members; the most important adhesions included Engineers, Miners, Shipwrights and all the building crafts. The Council participated in shorter hours agitations, in a strike of painters, and in arbitration of a weavers' dispute; it advocated courts of conciliation, supported projects for a free library and a civic museum, and arranged lectures by Sir Archibald Alison, the Sheriff and Tory historian.

Two of its members addressed the meeting of the National Association for the Promotion of Social Science (founded by Brougham in imitation of the British Association) held in Glasgow in 1860. A. J. Hunter (baker) and William Caw (joiner) spoke on 'the Objects of Trade Unions, friendly, protective, educative'. Alexander Frazer, the Edinburgh blacksmith, refuted the arguments of Peter Allan, a working man, that trade unions were 'injurious to the welfare of the community'. At the 1880 gathering in Edinburgh, a Workingmen's Meeting was held in the Assembly Hall, addressed by leading members of the Association; in moving a vote of thanks, James Thom, Trades Council president, affirmed that 'workmen did not strike for love of striking'.

The Glasgow Council adopted new rules in April 1867. At this date, it shared in the agitations for franchise extension and for amendment of the Master and Servant Act. In the latter, it had the collaboration of Lord Elcho, a Tory M.P. of social sympathies, who ultimately introduced the Bill of 1867 which satisfied much of their demands. About 1870, sixty-two trades were represented, covering some 14,000 workers. The Council had a Parliamentary Bills Committee, but did not intervene in trade disputes.

Matthew Lawrence, an early secretary, removed to London, where he was associated with the 'First International'. Andrew Boa, a mason, chairman in 1873, a founder of the Kinning Park Co-operative Society, and advocate of working-class Parliamentary representation, emigrated to Australia in 1875, and died there two years later.

In 1873 the Council co-operated with the Scottish National Education League (which stood for public as against ecclesiastical control) in running candidates at the first School Board election, but without success. Edward Caird, the moral philosopher, and James Borrowman, first manager of the S.C.W.S., were among the nominees. In 1875 it claimed to represent 26 trades with 10,000 members.

In 1878 the Council undertook an appeal to the Court of Session against the award of £100 damages to a local firm of glassmakers from a unionist who had seduced blacklegs from their employment; subscriptions to cover the cost produced a surplus. A successful verdict provided an important interpretation of the 1871 Act. In 1879 a conference of representatives of 33 trades was held on successive Saturdays under the Council's auspices; *inter alia*, the legal enactment of an 8-hour day was discussed, but was rejected by a two-to-one majority.

In Aberdeen, a 'Delegate Committee of Sympathy', with a regular constitution, subscriptions, etc., was established in May 1846, in consequence of a strike of joiners, and existed for about three years. From 1856 annual meetings of trade delegates were held regarding the midsummer holiday. A more enduring Council dates from 1868, on the initiative of the Joiners. Its early records were lost or destroyed by the secretary, for which he was censured by the Council. It met fortnightly, and unlike the others gave active support in trade disputes. In 1870 it took up the repeal of the Game Laws, and in 1877 its president, Thomas Gill, took part in the usual meetings for workers held in connection with the Social Science Congress. It gave much attention to municipal matters such as the police board, gasworks and free library.

A United Trades Council was formed in Dundee in December 1867; meetings were held quarterly. It corresponded with Edinburgh regarding trade union legislation. It was represented at the Trade Union Congress of 1875, and again in 1881, when the credentials of its delegate James Tyndall were challenged. He was one of a small number charged with being paid agents of Protectionist manufacturers, in this case the Greenock sugar interest. He claimed to be financed by a Council of 16 members representing 1400 trade unionists.

The present Council claims continuity only from 1885.

Councils also came into being in the 'seventies in Paisley (1874) and Greenock. The latter enjoyed the services as secretary of Matthew Allan of the Operative Masons.

These Trades Councils were frequently active in the national sphere. Glasgow was responsible for the formation of a Committee for the Repeal of the Master and Servant Act, at a conference of trade representatives in April 1864. Next month this body was constituted a national executive to co-ordinate the campaign; it met fortnightly. George Newton, a potter, apparently a small master or independent craftsman, who died on 4th January

1867 at the age of 36, and then secretary of the Council, acted as secretary of this committee; the chairman was Alexander Campbell.

A Memorandum was drawn up by a legal adviser, who was commissioned to draft a Bill.

The Glasgow Council took the initiative in convening a national congress in London in May 1864. Of that summoned by George Potter of the 'Beehive' in March 1867, its own secretary, John Proudfoot, acted as secretary, while the Council subscribed to the expenses. From this Edinburgh officially held aloof, though Troup, its chairman, attended. After the institution in 1868 of an annual Trades Union Congress, Scottish councils as well as individual unions were frequently represented, Edinburgh regularly from 1871. The Congress met in Glasgow in 1875, when mass demonstrations and a public banquet were held. At least three prominent Scots sat on the Parliamentary Committee in its early years—Alexander Macdonald, John Battersby and Andrew Boa. The latter was also chairman of a Criminal Law Amendment Repeal Association, set up to secure modification of the unsatisfactory trade union legislation of 1871. Glasgow Trades Council organised a West of Scotland demonstration on 1st November 1873, attended in drenching rain by 20,000. The Council protested against the Report of the subsequent Commission (1875) and Dundee Council thanked Macdonald, who was a member, for his Minority Report.

Some attempts were made to establish a Scottish organisation. In July 1856, a meeting of Trades Delegates in Glasgow appointed a committee to 'draw up a code for a Scottish Federation of United Trades' to 'promote the interests and ameliorate the conditions of the industrious classes'; John Proudfoot was again secretary. The constitution was approved by later gatherings, apparently without practical result. In 1860-61 a scheme for a federal union of trades was discussed by Edinburgh and Glasgow Councils, but was rejected. It proposed the division of Scotland into six industrial districts, with an annual conference and a system of arbitration for trade disputes, and assistance by a levy in authorised strikes and lockouts. Some such scheme was periodically revived within the next twenty years. In February 1870, a national conference was held in Edinburgh, lasting three days, and attended by delegates from Dundee and Glasgow as well as from local bodies. Several papers on trade union topics were read, and industrial legislation was discussed. A more permanent organisation was essayed in 1872, at the instance of the Glasgow Council, when a delegate conference formed a United Trades Confederation of Scotland and adopted rules. Peter Henrietta, a tailor and ex-Chartist, a leading member of Glasgow Council, became chairman, and Charles Laing, a Glasgow baker, secretary. Its object was 'to render all moral and pecuniary assistance to trades connected with the association'. The officers, executive, and 'judicial council' were to be subject to the 'delegate conference and votes of members'. The executive was to levy affiliated societies proportionately to their membership, in order to meet claims for benefit in trades disputes.

This body later in the year took up the cause of compositors dismissed by *The Scotsman* after a notable strike, but seems not to have long survived, presumably because of the depression.

Several cases came before the Scottish courts during these years, in which rather conflicting interpretations of the legal position of trade unions were given. Arbroath Small Debt Court in January 1869 denied the capacity of a trade union to sue or to be sued, as an 'illegal body in restraint of trade'. At Perth Sheriff Court, an attempt by the Masons' Union to recover arrears of subscriptions from a local lodge was dismissed; while the Airdrie Sheriff held illegal, action taken to exclude non-unionists from employment. These cases were discussed in the *Journal of Jurisprudence* for 1873. In the test cases of *Shanks* v. *The Operative Masons* (1870) and *McKernan* v. *the Same* (1874), claims on the benefit fund for compensation were rejected on the ground that they could not be enforced by the court.

In a case already mentioned—*James Couper & Sons, Flintglass-makers, Glasgow* v. *Robert Macfarlane*, the Court of Session (February 1879) overturned the verdict of the Sheriff, who had awarded damages to the firm for alleged seduction of employees to break their contract of service. The men involved had been imported from England to supply the place of locked-out workers. Proceedings were twice adjourned to obtain production of the books of the Flint Glass Cutters' Mutual Protective Association, whose headquarters were in Birmingham; George Quin, secretary for the Glasgow district, and other officials were cited as witnesses. The evidence was conflicting, and the verdict was virtually one of 'not proven'; if the fact of enticement had been proved, the defendant would have been held liable for damages.

Scottish trade unionism as a whole was thus largely submerged once more by economic disaster, but alike in the specialised unions of the principal industries and in the general organisation of localities, it was now sufficiently strong to maintain in most cases at least a bare existence, and to revive under happier auspices.

The characteristic features of the period may be summarised as follows. The Scottish unions shared in the distinctive traits of 'Model Unionism'. Growing approximation and inter-relationship of English and Scottish industrial conditions is reflected in organisation and policy. Some of the unions, especially in heavy industry, were British rather than English or Scottish. Among features of policy are the pressure exerted on existing political parties and on representatives for legislation of special trade union concern, advocacy of franchise extension, and support of subsidised emigration as a means of curtailing the labour market. A general acceptance of the classical economics and of private enterprise may be assumed. The chief indication of a more militant attitude was the shorter hours agitation of the early 'seventies.

From such casual evidence as is available, it may be added that the leaders, at any rate, of trade unionism were thoroughly 'respectable' figures, frequently active churchmen of temperate and puritanical habits, with a high degree of literacy, attested, for example, by the literal readability of their copperplate calligraphy, and appearing in their photographs in typical Victorian garb.

Owenite Socialism was indeed not dead. Alexander Campbell remained its consistent and sanguine champion until his death in 1870, and by him and other supporters, such as 'Parson' James Adams, a spokesman of the later phase of Chartism, experiments in producers' societies were initiated in the 'fifties and 'sixties—e.g. Tailors and Hatters in Glasgow (1850), Painters (1860), Coopers (1865). Except in a few examples in building, the only permanent achievement however was the widespread formation during this period of local consumers' co-operative societies, some of which, such as St. Cuthbert's (Edinburgh) and Kinning Park (Glasgow), rapidly attained commercial success, though the Utopian ideal soon became merely a theme for perorations. A Scottish Co-operative Wholesale Society, controlled by representatives of retail societies, was founded in 1868, and established factories for furniture, soap and other domestic commodities, as well as undertaking wholesale and import activities.

The quarter of a century between 1850 and 1875 was an epoch of rising standards of life, due largely to increasing output and expanding markets. The fruits of growing prosperity were unequally shared; the skilled worker in full employment benefited, in part at least, through trade union organisation, but the mass of unskilled casual labour lagged behind. Then set in the 'Great Depression', a term whose validity is now disputed, but which seems justified at any rate with reference to industrial Scotland in the late 'seventies and early 'eighties. It may be attributed mainly to the first real onset of foreign competition, especially from the now united Germany and post-Civil War U.S.A.; thus Britain's supremacy as the 'workshop of the world' was challenged, as is reflected in the revival of Protectionist proposals. Scottish industry was already so ill-balanced, so much concentrated on the heavy industries of the Clyde, that here the effects were most serious. The decade 1875-85 witnessed so thorough a setback to Scottish trade unionism that its revival in the later 'eighties may be regarded as opening a new phase.

POLITICAL ACTIVITIES

A note may be added on political activities. Just prior to its reorganisation, Edinburgh Trades Council affiliated (February 1867) to the Scottish National Reform League, formed in September 1866 and associated with a similar body in London with an identical programme. Councillor John Burt of Glasgow later noted as a 'Land Taxer', became chairman of the League. A Glasgow Reform Union, of which Newton was secretary, merged in the Scottish body; William Troup was chairman of the Edinburgh branch (1867). Several unions, notably the Tailors, took part in a procession and demonstration under its auspices in October 1866. A Democratic Hall at Trongate, Glasgow, was its headquarters. Dr. Gavin Clark, afterwards leader of the Crofters, conducted a 'Radical Electoral Association' in the 'sixties. Peter Henrietta of the Trades Council figured in a 'Republican Association' about 1870.

A meeting of the Reform League's General Council with a Glasgow Workingmen's Association in September 1869 called a conference to prepare a municipal programme; Bailie Moir, the ex-Chartist, participated. Glasgow Trades Council was divided on a proposal to seek independent labour representation; by a majority vote, a Committee to further this was set up in 1873, with little practical result. Two trade union candidates in Glasgow and one in Edinburgh (John McWhinnie in Canongate) unsuccessfully stood at Town Council elections in November of that year.

Conservative Workingmen's Associations existed in Edinburgh and Glasgow from the 'seventies; the latter was addressed in 1872 by George Troup, a former Radical journalist, who had become an Imperialist and Protectionist.

There is little indication of a definite connection of Scottish trade unionism with the movement for Parliamentary representation active in England at the time. For the election of 1868, the first after enfranchisement of many urban workers, a questionnaire was drawn up for submission to candidates; it embraced fifteen points, including legal security for trade unions, amendment of the Master and Servant Act, a national system of education and nationalisation of railways. Alexander Macdonald came forward as a candidate for Kilmarnock in 1868, but retired before the poll; this is the sole instance of a working-class Parliamentary candidature in Scotland between the collapse of Chartism and the emergence of Land Reform and Socialist spokesmen in the 'eighties.

The *Sentinel*, published weekly in Glasgow from 1850 to 1877, was founded by the Owenite Robert Buchanan (father of the poet) and William Love (1810-65), whose bookseller's shop was a Radical 'howff'; it was afterwards controlled by Alexander Macdonald and edited for a time by Alexander Campbell. It featured trade union news and voiced labour opinion. A file preserved at Colindale is an invaluable source of information for this period.

The Edinburgh Mechanics' Subscription Library was founded in March 1825. Henry Rankin, an upholsterer, on the staff of the *Express*, was, while its president, arrested for his Chartist activities in 1848; he was later secretary (1855-59). There were a few similar institutions elsewhere, e.g. at Perth, less under 'middle class' control than was common with the Mechanics' Institutes. The Edinburgh Letterpress Printers had their own library in the 1850's. A catalogue exists.

CHAPTER IV

THE LATE VICTORIAN PERIOD

WHILE some unions succumbed under the crisis, most preserved their continuity, though in an enfeebled condition. The ulterior consequences in some measure contributed to their revival, in so far as prolonged unemployment and distress stimulated the rise of agitation and propaganda, frequently with a Socialist tinge. No such sensational developments as the Matchworkers' and Dock strikes and Trafalgar Square riots which ushered in the so-called 'New Unionism' (a term now blown upon) in England are apparent, but there were towards the end of the century considerable extensions both of range and activity, local and national. At the same time, a relative stability in industrial life was maintained.

By way of introduction, the main features which demand consideration may be indicated.

1. The recovery of unionism in the older types of industry, and the beginnings of federal unity among them.
2. The initiation of organisation among women workers.
3. The growth of unionism in heavy industry, and the relative prominence of this section in the movement.
4. Tendencies to joint action, especially in the political sphere.

The trade unions prominent in earlier periods had been chiefly those associated with housing, clothing and other small-scale consumptional enterprise. They had, in the main, sometimes after a rather spectacular rise in the middle 'sixties, crumbled away into what were at best sporadic local groups. In the 'eighties and 'nineties there was a marked revival, and a tendency to federal organisation becomes manifest.

The Scottish Typographical Association was little affected by depression; indeed, litigation is said at its height to have increased the demand for the services of its members. Despite disputes with the newspaper press over machinery and female labour, it maintained a high degree of organisation, and enforced seven-years apprenticeship. The consent of the executive was required for a strike. A 'fair list' was issued in 1895. Membership was about 3000. Robert Johnstone and John Eddy, secretaries respectively of the Scottish Association and the Glasgow branch, were the outstanding figures.

The Scottish National Operative Tailors' and Tailoresses' Association was also an efficient body. Reorganised in 1866, it held triennial conferences. Its membership rose to 3763 in 56 branches (1892), and its funds to £3300. In the 'eighties it carried on an active campaign against sweating, on which a pamphlet (1880) was issued by Neil McLean, its leading spokesman; the support of the Sabbath Alliance and other religious bodies was sought. An inquiry by a House of Lords Committee was obtained. Chronic disputes with the English union continued, especially as to alleged mutual encroachments; the Scottish Trade Union Congress on its inception investigated the matter, and gave verdict that each society should confine itself within national bounds (1900).

In the baking trade, some local societies persisted after the *débâcle* of 1877. These combined in 1885-86, on the initiative of Alexander Catto (1850-1926) of Aberdeen, to form the Operative Bakers of Scotland National Federal Union; Oliver Gray (1843-1911), also of Aberdeen, was first president. Its main object was stated to be the restriction of working hours, to commence not earlier than 5 a.m. A national fund was to be raised by weekly assessments; branches could make their own levies; a Board of Supervision, to be migratory every two years, was to serve as executive. A Glasgow union, organised by Archibald Hunter (1820-1903), affiliated in 1888. The central body was registered in 1889, by which time it was fairly well established, thanks largely to the energy of the executive, then situated in Aberdeen, with Catto as chairman. A five-years apprenticeship was demanded, with the abolition of 'living in', enforcement of the 'closed shop' and a 55-hour week. In October 1889, a strike secured the latter in many areas, Edinburgh and Glasgow excepted. Many members, however, soon abandoned the union, because of a strike levy, and its achievements were dissipated; up to 70 hours a week were worked, and wages sometimes fell below £1 a week. Friction with co-operative societies was frequent—e.g. 1889-91 with St. Cuthbert's over night work. A legislative 8-hour day now became a regular demand, and bills embodying it were drafted. The insanitary conditions, especially of underground bakeries, were criticised, and excessive introduction of apprentices swamped the labour market. William G. Hunter (1857-1944) of Glasgow was appointed national organiser in 1897, when membership had attained 4500 in 46 branches. In conjunction with the Master Bakers' Association, an arbitration board was formed in October 1898, and an agreement drawn up, terminable at thirty days' notice, which prescribed a minimum wage of 28s., and 9d. an hour for overtime. A breakaway Protective Society, which yielded concessions to employers, had only temporary success, with a membership of 600.

Among the building trades, the Carpenters were the strongest, though still divided between the predominantly Scottish Associated and the predominantly English Amalgamated Society. The latter had 22 Scottish branches, with 1200 members on the Clyde (1891). The former, under the secretaryship of James Beveridge (1883-92) —who signalised his appointment by giving a rhymed address of reminiscence at an Edinburgh *soirée*—and of William McIntyre (1892-1902), made some advance in membership and wages in this period. It had increased its funds to £10,000 by 1891, and by the close of the century its membership had all but reached 10,000 in 174 branches. A Conciliation Board was formed in 1890. The union had chronic demarcation disputes with the Shipwrights—e.g. in September 1893, when both parties were locked out; a settlement was made by arbitration.

The Operative Masons' Union of Scotland had in 1892 60 branches and some 4000 members; this rose to 12,000 by the end of the century. The organisation was however weak and inefficient. From 1884 the Glasgow branch held annual conferences with the Master Masons' Association, at which standard rates for the ensuing year were fixed. A few years after the dissolution of the local branch, an independent Aberdeen Operative Masons' and Stone Cutters' Society existed from October 1888, under the leadership of James Annand, secretary of the Trades Council.

The Bricklayers had a small society for Glasgow and district; an Edinburgh Association was formed in 1890.

The Painters and Plasterers, after a period of disorganisation, were reunited on a federal basis. A Scottish National Federation of House and Ship Painters was established in Glasgow in November 1887; it was later known as the Scottish Painters' Society, with 25 branches in 1898, when George Greenhill of Edinburgh was president. Its Edinburgh branch had then about 500 members. An interdict was obtained against division of its funds by the Aberdeen branch (July 1900).

In 1888 the Scottish National Operative Plasterers' Federal Union was formed by local clubs. It remained very decentralised. In a few years it had about 1000 members. By agreement with the employers, it paid an inspector as a safeguard against scamped work, which had provoked a lockout. The union maintained five-years apprenticeship, and had a strike benefit of 12s. One of its founders, Daniel Baird (1861-1953), a 'Single Taxer' and pioneer of the Scottish Labour Party, was general secretary, 1906-37.

In 1891 the United Operative Plumbers' Association (1865) sustained a Scottish breakaway, when two lodges seceded. They were absorbed (1893) by the earlier secessionist body, the Operative Plumbers' Association of Scotland (1872), whose numbers were thereby raised from 300 to 700. The Scottish trade continued to be more conservative than the English, and more purely devoted to house building. The Scottish union had successful litigation with the English in 1896, but sometimes co-operated with it. The former retained the old method of a travelling seat of government; by 1900 it had over 1200 members and had secured a partial revival of apprenticeship. George Galloway, one of its officers, was appointed a factory inspector in 1893.

The Amalgamated Slaters' Society of Scotland apparently continued an uneventful and prosperous existence.

The Glasgow Operative Glaziers' Trade and Friendly Society was formed in 1891 by the amalgamation of the two local friendly societies, about twenty years old, in which employers had participated; the new body became definitely a trade union, and collaborated with other local societies. All of these, with the exception of Edinburgh, ultimately combined in the Operative Glaziers' Trade and Friendly Society with a membership of 400. Owing to the scattered nature of the work, much of the business was transacted by post; apprentices, numbering one in four, had a special section, and technical classes were arranged for them.

A Glasgow and Suburbs Building Trades Federation existed in 1896, and sought to establish an affiliated body in Edinburgh.

Total Scottish membership in the building trades was estimated by the Webbs in 1892 as about 25,000. In general, there was no marked development in the industry; wage rates were maintained, and an attitude of contentment prevailed. The prominence of the unions in the working-class movement was less than heretofore.

TEXTILE TRADES

In the textile trades, unionism continued to be weak, largely owing to the predominance of female labour. In cotton there survived the almost negligible minute associations of male skilled workers, such as the Society of Twisters and Drawers. A Scottish Bleachfield Workers' Union was formed in 1888 with headquarters in Dundee and the local heretical preacher, Rev. David Macrae, as honorary president, but reported only 130 members a decade later. This section of the industry was just coming under monopolistic English control. A Scottish Lace and Textile Union, formed in 1891 in the Darvel area of Ayrshire, where factory production was growing, later federated with the Amalgamated Society of Operative Lace Makers, formed in Nottingham in 1894.

In the woollen industry of the Borders, hitherto little affected, efforts at organisation were now made. A Hawick Power Loom Weavers' Society was formed in 1887, and drew up price scales. The tweed-mill workers of Galashiels were organised in 1895 by the National Union of Textile Workers from Yorkshire; the new union inherited £30 deposited in a local building society by the trustees of a former Weavers' Society which had existed about 40 years earlier. This 'English invasion', however, had but ephemeral success.

It was in the flax and kindred jute industries of the north-east that the most notable developments took place, virtually pioneering the effective organisation of women workers. An unsuccessful strike against wage reductions took place in the summer of 1875; exactly ten years later renewed cuts led to the formation of the Dundee Mill and Factory Operatives' Union. It was supported by the Women's Protective League; Rev. Henry Williamson (1839-1925), a Unitarian minister active on the School Board, became honorary president and exercised a benevolent dictatorship. Besides employees of jute works in Dundee (only 12 per cent of whom were male), the union included 500 linen workers in Perth, a group in Aberdeen, and a few in Arbroath, Brechin, Montrose, etc. It agitated for legal protection, and from 1888 provided accident and funeral, but no out-of-work or sick benefits. It published intermittently between 1885 and 1889 the *Mill & Factory Herald* at a halfpenny. Within a few years it accumulated nearly £2500, and claimed to have raised wages 30 per cent. In April 1893, with 3000 members and £3000 at its disposal, it called a strike against wage reductions, and owing to a breakaway among employers, the cut was restored.

In 1889 arose the Forfarshire Federal Union of Textile Workers, which, after a strike, obtained concessions, including a wage advance for lower-paid male workers. It soon evolved into the Scottish Mill and Factory Workers' Federal Union, which was organised as a loose combination of branches with local autonomy. Its strongholds were the smaller linen manufacturing burghs, Brechin, Forfar and Montrose, all in Forfarshire (now Angus). It soon had a membership of some 6000—about 50 per cent of all employees—of whom two-thirds were women. It had a subscription of 1d. per week; it favoured the abolition of half-time work for juveniles. At first there was antagonism between it and the Dundee union, but the latter became affiliated, as did the small organisation set up in Aberdeen in 1891 with the aid of the Trades Council. In 1899, when J. Rose of Forfar was secretary, and Councillor William Johnston of Aberdeen chairman, it supported jute-workers locked out in Aberdeen, but withheld support from the Dundee society during a strike in 1900. There were in Dundee very small unions of Calender Workers and of Bobbin and Shuttle Operatives.

In the Glasgow area also, sporadic attempts were made by enthusiasts to organise mill girls. At the instance of the Trades Council, the Scottish Weaving Factories Female Workers Industrial Union was formed in November 1888, with an initial enrolment of under 100. A year later, a branch which took the name of the Ayrshire Lasses Union, with about 200 members, developed out of a strike at Dalry, through which the millgirls obtained an increase of 1s. a week. In 1882 Aberdeen Trades Council sought to organise women textile operatives. By 1884 a Workwomen's Protective and Benefit Society sent delegates to the Council, but it did not survive the decade. There is casual reference as early as 1872 to an Edinburgh Upholsterers' Sewers Society, a union for women only.

The Women's Protective and Provident League formed a

branch in Glasgow in 1890, 200 strong, in which Mrs. E. G. Anderson was shortly succeeded as organising secretary by Miss Margaret H. Irwin. In 1895 was formed the Scottish Council for Women's Trades, a philanthropic body with influential spokesmen such as Rev. G. Adam Smith, afterwards principal of Aberdeen University. It existed until 1939, being dissolved on the resignation of Miss Irwin, who had been secretary throughout; she died soon after (January 1940). This body encouraged organisation among working women, and supported a strike in Bridgeton weaving factories against reduction of wages. Largely owing to the fear of victimisation, little success was attained.

The Council secured the affiliation of 16 trades councils and 27 trade unions, and was for some years represented at the Scottish Trades Union Congress. It conducted a campaign on behalf of women shop assistants; it twice investigated conditions of work in laundries, and pressed for their inclusion under the Factory Acts. In January 1899 a meeting under its auspices was held in Glasgow to promote women's trade unionism, Rev. M. P. Laughlin, secretary of the Glasgow Christian Social Union presiding, with Miss Irwin and John Wilson of the Shaleworkers speaking.

Mention is made of an Aberdeen Union of Women Workers, with the Countess of Aberdeen as president (February 1899).

THE HEAVY INDUSTRIES

We turn to the heavy industries, which had become the mainstay of Scottish economic life. The prominence of the miners' unions and their initiative in the political sphere are notable features. In these respects indeed they had already distinguished themselves in the time of Alexander Macdonald, but with the early years of the ninth decade, all organisation had virtually crumbled away. The Fife and Kinross Association (1869) alone preserved its continuity, 80 per cent strong, under the skilled guidance of John Weir, secretary from 1881 to 1908.

By 1886 organisation was reviving in other areas. Midlothian miners have a regular union with records from October 1886. In January 1888, a separate East Lothian Association was formed; the two counties definitely amalgamated their associations in August 1889. A paid agentship was established three months later, and combined with the secretaryship; these posts were for many years (1891-1917) held by Robert Brown of Newbattle, who became provost of Dalkeith. A Conciliation Board was formed in 1891. Membership was about 3000 at the end of the century.

Clackmannanshire had a small but steady union, closely associated with that of Fife.

The western counties were less prosperous and stable. In Ayrshire a union was formed in November 1883, and two agents were appointed; but resuscitation was required in August 1886, when Keir Hardie became the principal official, at a fee of £75. Actively associated with him were John Banks and Bailie John Brown of Galston, both blacklisted for their labours. Peter Muir (1850-1911) was secretary, 1884-1908; James Brown of Annfield, afterwards M.P., became president.

In Lanarkshire also there were sporadic mass meetings, at one of which, in October 1883, Hector McNeil of Larkhall was appointed as paid agent to organise the county. Again in April 1886 a County Union was formally constituted, with William Small, formerly a draper's assistant (1849-1902), as secretary. This too virtually collapsed within two or three years. Blantyre, 1000 strong, alone remained effectively organised, though Motherwell and Larkhall were intermittently active, under the leadership respectively of Robert Steele, a veteran with over half a century's experience in the pits, and of Robert Smillie. Under the latter's chairmanship, the County Union revived in the early 'nineties. He retained office for many years and Small was reappointed agent in October 1892. A Central Board met weekly at Hamilton.

Stirlingshire, often styled the Forth and Clyde Association (1886), was dominated by Robert Chisholm Robertson (1860-1930), originally a mining engineer, who from an office in Glasgow conducted numerous public activities. It was eventually expelled from the federation for failure to pay dues. Dunbartonshire was not effectively organised on a county basis until late in the 'nineties. West Lothian coal-miners were organised, if at all, mainly in the shale-workers' union (Scottish Miners and Oilworkers, 1886).

A national federation was nominally revived in 1886 with R. Chisholm Robertson as chairman, Keir Hardie as secretary, and Weir of Fife as treasurer. From 25,000 to 40,000 miners were nominally represented, but the organisation had only a shadowy existence, consisting chiefly in delegate conferences, with no power to bind members. It fostered the formation of county unions, and in May 1887 appointed a national organiser, William Bullock of Midlothian. After a disastrous strike in the spring of 1887, a 10-day working fortnight, a legislative 8-hour day, and the nationalisation of royalties were accepted as the official policy. At first associated with the National Union of Miners—the creation of Macdonald—the Scottish body joined the rival Miners Federation of Great Britain on its formation in 1888.

In 1893 greater activity developed; successive strikes enforced some advance in wages. The prevalence of sectionalism led to agitation for closer unity, reinforced by pressure from England. After negotiations among the districts, a constitution was adopted in March 1894, and henceforth a Scottish Miners' Federation existed on a county basis. The tendency was towards centralisation and levelling of conditions, though progress was rendered slow by local differences, especially those of psychology, between the hereditary miners of Fife and the Lothians and the heterogeneous incomers of the later-developed western coalfields, with their less stable organisations. Breakaways sometimes occurred, partly through controversies in which the protagonist was Chisholm Robertson, on his return from a sojourn in South Africa. For some years he ran a rival Central Miners' Association, with three to four thousand members, and was ultimately expelled from the trade union movement. He went to Australia, and still later set up business in Glasgow, where he died in March 1930, having published fundamentalist and anti-socialist tracts. Smillie as chairman and Brown of Midlothian as secretary held office for some twenty years; this partnership of east and west contributed much to the advance of the Federation. In the national strike of June to October 1894, some 70,000 participated. After prolonged deliberations, a Scottish Coalfields Conciliation Board was formed in January 1908; a membership of about 50,000 was recorded at this date.

Some shale-miners in the Lothians, chiefly in the Calders area, had been organised with colliers in a short-lived union in the time of Macdonald. In May 1886 was formed the Mid and West Lothian Miners' Association, afterwards termed the Scottish Shale-miners Association. It was long dominated by John Wilson, a Broxburn shale-miner, secretary from its inception to his death in 1912. In 1887 and 1889 the union had bitter and protracted conflicts with the oil companies, organised in the Scottish Mineral Oil Association. It was able to reduce hours from an average of 10½ or 11 to 9 per day, and to obtain the appointment of check-weighmen and observance of the Employers' Liability Act. It operated as a district of the Scottish Miners' Federation, with occasional lapses owing to Wilson's independent policy, but eventually drew apart from the coal-miners and towards the oil refinery workers.

Some ironstone-miners were apparently organised by the Ayrshire Miners' Federation about 1900.

The definitive establishment of trade unionism among iron and steelworkers was a further notable advance of the period. Here there was almost a caste distinction among operatives, to some extent hereditary. The more highly skilled and responsible jobs obtained relatively high remuneration at the cost of long hours; the unskilled were performed by more casual labour, virtually employed by the 'first hands', acting as subcontractors. After a setback sustained in the 'seventies by the Associated Society of Iron and Steelworkers, a North of Scotland organisation, unionism was virtually extinct; the chief employers in the industry, such as the Bairds and the Neilsons, were strong opponents of workers' combination. From 1871 there were, however, regular consultations regarding wage rates, and these preserved industrial peace. About 1883 a demand developed for separate Scottish regulation, but the formation of a union was deferred.

In January 1886, as the result of a strike at Motherwell against worsened conditions, the British Steel Smelters' Amalgamated Association was established. Under the guidance as secretary of John Hodge, later a cabinet minister, who published his reminiscences *From Workman's Cottage to Windsor Castle*, it sought peaceful and ordered relations with employers, and was encouraged by James Riley, long manager of the Steel Company of Scotland. Within five years it had about 3000 members, and obtained substitution of direct employment for the contracting system. It soon spread to South Wales and in 1892 transferred its headquarters to Manchester. The previous year it held its annual three-day conference in Glasgow, attended by 41 delegates, of whom 10 were Scottish; Robert Dunlop of Motherwell presided.

The Associated Society of Millmen, also of strike origin, was formed in February 1888 to cater for grades not covered by the former union, which declined overtures for unity. It enrolled 2000 members in its first year, and banked £2000. It soon adopted the name of the Amalgamated Society of Steel and Iron Workers, and co-operated with the employers in setting up a Board of Conciliation for the Manufactured Steel Trade of the West of Scotland (1890). Its moving spirit was John Cronin, a stocktaker at Hallside Works, secretary from 1889 to 1903.

These unions, though successful in maintaining rates of pay, failed to reduce long hours or abolish Sunday labour. Twelve-hour shifts were worked until the end of the First World War. The usual harmony was broken by a twelve months' strike at Mossend Steelworks (1899-1900). Little was achieved for the subordinate unskilled labour, paid by the day.

These unions were local in the sense that the Scottish iron and steel industry was almost confined to the Clyde area. This, the industrial hub of Scotland, was also, though not so exclusively, the centre of shipbuilding and engineering, and the corresponding unions had thus the bulk of their membership there. These industries, of relatively recent growth, were rather unorganised. Able and independent employers, many of the self-made type, ruled autocratically. The prevalence of piecework and of sub-contracting also militated against unity. In the early 'nineties there were in this category about a hundred unions, mostly small and uninfluential. The greatest, the Engineers and the Boilermakers, were centralised British unions; the Scottish organisation consisted only in branches, with consequent friction.

The Amalgamated Society of Engineers, still essentially a benefit society of the 'New Model' species, had over 8000 Scottish members, some 10 per cent of the total employed. A 54-hour week was common, wages in 1886 averaged 26s. and had not increased on balance within twenty years; they improved considerably in the next decade. A five-years apprenticeship was served. In November 1895 the Clyde Employers' Association locked out 3000 engineers, acting in conjunction with those in Belfast; after three months a compromise was reached. The general strike of 1897 was precipitated by a lockout of 35 per cent of the membership of the A.S.E. and associated unions, enforced by employers in retaliation for a strike in London in support of an

8-hour day. The Clyde members, now 6500 in 23 branches, had not been enthusiastic for that reform, but regarded the employers' action as a threat to unionism, and withdrew their labour almost solidly. The dispute commenced in July, and dragged on till early in the New Year, resulting in a defeat for the union, which was at the end of its resources. However, a speedy recovery was made, and the episode heralded a new era in engineering unionism.

The United Patternmakers' Association, formed in 1872, had its seat of government in Glasgow from 1884 to 1891. It had then about 1600 members, which, however, included less than one-third of the trade in the Glasgow area, although a wage advance was obtained, making the average about 33s. William Mosses, who afterwards wrote a rather incoherent history of the union, was secretary from 1884 to 1917. A separate Associated Patternmakers of Scotland Society was formed in Falkirk for the light castings industry, with the approval of the parent society; in September 1896 it had only some 200 members.

The Associated Blacksmiths, a Scottish organisation formed in 1857, had little over 2000 members, with John Thomson as general secretary. Both piece and time rates were common, and no minimum had been secured; a five-years apprenticeship was usual.

The long-established Society of Boilermakers and Iron Shipbuilders (1832), which had been strongly represented in Scotland since the 'fifties, sustained a secession in Glasgow in September 1886, as the result of a dispute about the administration of the Society, and the 'high-handed action of the executive', dominated by the very efficient secretary, Robert Knight; the conduct of the local delegate on the Clyde, E. Rothwell, had also occasioned friction. The Scottish Boilermakers' Society was thus founded, but survived only about three years. In the summer of 1891, about 5000 boilermakers on the Clyde struck against a 5 per cent wage cut which had been accepted by the executive; they were supported by 24 out of 43 Scottish branches, but only by one-sixth of those in the rest of the British Isles. The strike continued for about seven weeks without Society benefit, but with the aid of local subscriptions administered by a strike committee; eventually unconditional surrender was accepted by an overwhelming vote. A wage regulation agreement was, however, maintained. Scottish membership was then nearly 8000, having doubled in a few years.

The Associated Shipwrights' Society, reconstituted in 1882, is described as 'compact but inert'. The average wage was 30s., payment was chiefly on time rates; tradesmen enjoyed a 54-hour week and a 5-years apprenticeship. The Glasgow District had 'Dock Rules and Bylaws for the Port of Glasgow', prescribing normal working hours; an 'understood rate of wages was recognised'. In 1888 there were 34 branches, one-half in Scotland; the Glasgow membership was about 3000. Alexander Wilkie (1850-1928), afterwards the first Scottish Labour M.P. (Dundee, 1906-18), was long secretary; the headquarters were transferred to Newcastle-on-Tyne in 1887. A Shipyard Labourers' Union was formed in Govan in May 1894.

Two other unions may be included in the heavy industries group—one a veteran, the other a newcomer to Scotland. The Associated Society of Ironmoulders of Scotland, which had an unbroken record from 1831, had a relatively large membership, about 6000 in 1890, 7200 in 1899, when its funds approximated £50,000. It made little attempt to regulate working conditions; two-thirds were on time rates, at 7d. an hour; a 56-hour week was worked. James M. Jack (1848-1912) was secretary from about 1880; he served on the Parliamentary Committee of the Trades Union Congress and on Glasgow City Council. Rules were revised in 1897, a Scottish executive and assistant secretary, John Brown, a Co-operator and I.L.P.-er, were appointed.

In April 1889 the Central Ironmoulders' Association was formed, mainly for unskilled workers; it was chiefly confined to the light castings industry of the Falkirk district, and had a membership of 2500 to 3000. The subscription was 6d. a week; John Waddell was secretary. It was for years at feud with the older body, which declined to recognise it as a *bona fide* union. However, they sometimes collaborated, and joined with the Brassmoulders and other ten unions in a Federation of Moulders and Collateral Trades in 1905.

Local societies, federated as the Scottish Operative Brassfounders, amalgamated as the Scottish Brassmoulders' Union in 1888.

The National Association of Blastfurnacemen established an effective organisation in Scotland in 1889-90, with about 1000 members, and Charles Vickers as agent. Wages were then from 10s. to 15s. a day, but men on the average worked only three or four days per week. A strike began in October 1890, in support of a demand for the abolition of Sunday labour, or its payment at time and a half rates. The employers kept the furnaces idle for eighteen weeks, then attempted resumption with non-union labour, and threatened to evict strikers from company-owned houses. Under this pressure, the strike was abandoned after an uneventful course of twenty-three weeks; a reduction of 20 per cent in wages was enforced, on the plea of falling prices of the product.

These unions had in 1892 a Scottish membership of about 45,000, principally in the Glasgow area, and numbered about one-third of the trade unionists in Scotland, as compared with one-sixth in England. Some, including the Boilermakers, Pattern-makers and Shipwrights, joined the Federation of Engineering and Shipbuilding Trades formed in 1890 at the instance of Robert Knight; in practice its main function was the settlement of inter-union disputes. The frequent close connection with, if not absorption in, English unions illustrates the growing unification of English and Scottish industry, as does the occasional case of a union of Scottish origin expanding southward and ultimately centring south of the Border. The exclusiveness of the better established unions, and their disregard of the subordinate unskilled and usually unorganised labourers was noted by the Webbs, who investigated the situation at this date; their policy may generally be described as conservative, adhering to mid-Victorian ideals of 'Model Unionism'.

The advance of unionism among those employed in various forms of transport is a further kindred feature, attributable in part to the growing importance of communications in the economic life of the nation. Railways had meantime an unquestioned dominance on land, and the indiscriminate and competitive planlessness of their early career had given place to a measure of combination. With them is connected the most dramatic episode of this period, comparable with the London Dock Strike.

Railwaymen were still divided between the Scottish Society of Railway Servants formed in Glasgow in 1872, and the Amalgamated Society of England, Scotland, Ireland and Wales, which had established several branches in Scotland. The excessive hours usually worked were responsible for considerable agitation—

e.g. a meeting in Aberdeen in January 1882, when demands for shorter hours were supported by the Lord Provost and by a parish minister of Radical views. A short and partial strike in 1883 elicited a few disappointing concessions. Under the secretaryship from 1886 of Henry Tait, afterwards chairman of Glasgow Trades Council, and a town councillor there, the Scottish Society increased its membership to 6700 by the spring of 1890; the English Society reported steady progress, and an 'amicable understanding . . . not to encroach' was concluded. In November 1889, a demand was presented to the companies, of which the main points were: a 10-hour day, overtime pay, annual holidays and a guaranteed week's work. After long delays, the companies finally declined arbitration (October to November 1890). Congestion due to the opening of the Forth Bridge made grievances more acute, and against the advice of the executive, mass meetings on the initiative of Glasgow declared for a general strike a few days before Christmas. The unions now co-operated, 8500 men came out forthwith, traffic was paralysed and public works stopped. Despite the inconvenience, there was much popular sympathy, voiced by such public spokesmen as Principal Rainy, and subscriptions came in to the amount of £1320. Strikers were evicted from Company houses; this evoked disturbances, e.g. at Motherwell. A civil suit was raised by the North British Railway Co. for damages against the Scottish union. Soon after New Year 1891, some services were restored, as men gradually returned to work, but a number held out till the end of January. Through the mediation of Lord Aberdeen and R. B. Haldane, a settlement was made. Litigation was abandoned, thus precluding a Scottish anticipation of the Taff Vale Judgment; investigation within a fortnight of grievances, and reinstatement as far as possible were promised. The North British and Caledonian Railway Companies, after conferring with representatives of their own employees, within a few months announced considerable concessions. A Select Committee of the House of Commons made elaborate inquiries into the working conditions of railwaymen, and largely substantiated their allegations.

The Scottish Society was however so weakened that it had to accept incorporation by the Amalgamated Society of Railway Servants of its remaining membership of about 1000 (August 1892); two of its officials were appointed Scottish organisers.

A fragment, some 500 strong, formed a Scottish Railwaymen's Union, with James Paisley of Glasgow, displaced by the amalgamation, as organiser; this body retained the funds and books of the old society, and at its first delegate meeting in December recorded nine branches. In 1895, however, it had to come to terms with the English General Railway Workers' Union (formed 1889, mainly of unskilled workers, and absorbed in the N.U.R. in 1913), which accepted its members as individuals, to avoid responsibility for a debt of £20 left by the union at its dissolution.

The Society of Locomotive Engineers and Firemen also got a foothold in Scotland, establishing a branch in Glasgow in 1891. A provisional agreement among the railway societies in November 1890, with a view to amalgamation or federation, was not ratified.

The National Amalgamated Sailors' and Firemen's Union, founded by Havelock Wilson in 1887, soon reached Scotland, where it enrolled 7500 members on the Clyde, and carried on a series of unsuccessful strikes; in 1891, it accepted the 'ticket' of the Employers' Federation.

An organisation which became a branch of the National Union of Dock Labourers was formed in Glasgow in February 1889 by Richard McGhee, afterwards an Irish Nationalist M.P. It entered into competition with the old established Glasgow Harbour Labourers' Union (1853) which made common cause with the employers against the intruder, at first with success, but was ultimately crushed out. Thus two of the chief examples of the 'New Unionism' obtained a permanent footing, especially on the Clyde.

As regards road transport, the Glasgow Carters had a union dating from about 1874, which was virtually a friendly society, with an entry fee of 3s. and weekly payments of 6d. A Scottish Horsemen's Union was formed in 1889, but seems not to have survived. John Urquhart, described as general secretary of the Association of Carters, was a Glasgow municipal candidate in 1894. In October 1898, the Scottish Carters' Association was formed—or revived—with John Simpson as secretary; it included workers formerly organised in the Railway Union, and was joined by some members of the Glasgow and other local societies.

Edinburgh cabdrivers had their own association; and in the spring of 1889, on the initiative of the Trades Council, a local Tramway Servants Association was formed. A Glasgow Drivers' and Conductors', or Glasgow Tramway Servants', Association, a benefit society, existed in 1884. In 1899 a Scottish Hackney Carriage and Tramway Employees Union formed a branch in Aberdeen.

A miscellaneous collection of other unions are known only from casual references. As regards agriculture, an attempt was again made, under the auspices of Aberdeen Trades Council, to organise farm servants; a union thus established in 1886, with J. C. Thompson, formerly president of the Council, as secretary, was active for some years in that area; it included carters, and the Aberdeen branch eventually merged in the General Workers' Union. A Scottish Ploughmen's Federal Union, centring in Perth, had most of its strength in that locality, with branches also in Paisley and in Ross-shire; Robert Duncan was secretary (*c.* 1890). It absorbed the remnants of the Aberdeenshire union (1895) and at its peak claimed 60,000 members, but was dissolved in 1900. It was mainly a benefit society, but sought a weekly half-holiday and abolition of long-term engagements.

A Glasgow and District Brewery Workers' Union was formed about 1889, and rejected affiliation to the Knights of Labour. About the same date, Glasgow Trades Council sought to form a National Union of Paper Workers. A Scottish Saw Mill Operatives and Woodcutting Machinemen's Society was formed in 1897; at its third annual meeting, William McCracken presiding, an increased membership was reported. A United Engine Keepers' Association of Scotland, with Thomas B. Anderson of Uddingston as general secretary, is mentioned in 1900. A Sewing Machine, Cycle and Toolmakers' Society held its fourth annual meeting in February 1894, with 120 paid-up members; complaints of apathy were made, but a proposal to dissolve was defeated.

In the furnishing trades, a ten months' dispute was settled; piecework was conceded, and prices mutually agreed by collective bargaining (January 1899). A Scottish Power Loom Carpet Trade Protective and Provident Association is mentioned in February 1893.

A Scottish Union of General Labourers held an organising meeting in Glasgow in February 1895. The Amalgamated Postal and Telegraph Benefit Society, founded in 1894, established an Edinburgh branch in December. After ten years it had over

11,000 members. The Postal Clerks' Association formed Scottish branches, and held its annual conference in Glasgow in 1901.

A Scottish Shopkeepers' and Assistants' Union, with John Frazer as secretary, had some success with an early-closing movement about 1890.

A Scottish District of the Knights of Labour, the American organisation, was established in July 1889; 12 'Assemblies' were formed, with about 3000 members; one at Ardrossan had 80 members. J. Shaw Maxwell, a lithographer and I.L.P. pioneer, became 'District Master Workman'. The organisation survived in Great Britain only a few years.

A Conference to promote better relations between Co-operators and trade unionists was held in Glasgow in January 1893, Professor Henry Dyer presiding. Papers were read by representatives of each.

JOINT ACTION

The expansion of organised joint action, on both a local and a national scale, is a notable feature of the period.

Trades Councils, as already described, had been established in the principal towns in the mid-Victorian epoch. That in Glasgow, formed in 1858, had now about 160 members, representing some 90 unions or branches. It promoted local organisation of trade unions, especially among women (as mentioned above), and co-operated in so doing with the Scottish Council for Women's Trades; it was also largely responsible for the creation of unions of Millmen, Painters, Seamen, Tramwaymen, Brewery and Distillery Workers. It supported such proposals as municipalisation of tramways, nationalisation of minerals and a legislative 8-hour day. It agitated against Sunday labour, and gave active assistance to the demands of the unemployed. In 1889 it arranged a course of lectures on 'Duties and Responsibilities as Citizens'. A Labour Bureau for Unemployed was opened by the Town Council in August 1890; John Warrington, ex-president of the Council, was appointed manager. A procession and demonstration were held in connection with the meeting of the Trades Union Congress in Glasgow in September 1892.

The Council in 1886 instituted a fund to support candidates for the Town Council, and after initial defeats secured several seats during the 'nineties, especially at the 'general' election of 1896 when five were won by candidates of the Workers' Municipal Committee, on which the Trades Council was represented; it received annual reports and endorsed candidates. Two labour members entered the School Board in 1894. Among the first councillors were Harry Tait of the Railwaymen (1888), John Cronin of the Millmen, and A. J. Hunter of the Bakers (1890), their secretary from 1883 to 1901. Other prominent figures in the Trades Council were George Carson, tinplate worker, afterwards secretary, John Eddy, printer, and Chisholm Robertson, the erratic miners' leader.

Edinburgh Council, reconstituted in 1867, also actively engaged in the furtherance of local unionism, having for the purpose set up in 1889 a Trade Organisation Committee. Over fifty trades were represented on the Council, among them unions as far afield as Broxburn Shaleminers and Hawick Weavers. The Council pursued an erratic course with regard to political action, the prevailing tendency being of the 'Lib-Lab' variety. It devoted much of its time to matters of municipal concern—e.g. housing, tramways, water supply; and also sought to intervene, not always with acceptance, in trade disputes, particularly where questions of demarcation were involved. A few candidates ran under its auspices for public bodies from 1893.

Eventually in 1899 the Edinburgh and Leith Workers' Municipal Committee, with thirty organisations affiliated, was formed to contest local elections. Outstanding members of the Council, included John Mallinson, representative of the Cordwainers (bootmakers), who was also for many years a Town Councillor, and a prominent Co-operator; David Blackburn, secretary of the Flint Glassmakers' Society, twice president; Neil McLean (d. 1895), secretary of the Tailors, secretary of the Council from 1880 to 1887, the first convener of the Trades Organisation Committee; and Thomas Wilson, the Bakers' secretary, appointed secretary of the Council in 1901. Charles Scott (d. 1892), a Tory advocate, sometimes assisted as legal adviser. A rare personal touch in the minutes is a vote of censure on an ex-president for alleged misconduct at a public banquet.

Dundee Council was re-formed in 1885. It soon won representation on local bodies, and paid representatives from its own funds. One of the first, Robert Bruce, died while president in 1892; he held seats on the School Board and Parish Council as well as the Town Council.

Aberdeen continued to assist affiliated unions in trade disputes, and supported the 8-hour movement. It established relief funds in periods of unemployment, and successfully pressed for municipal housing and a fair wages clause in public contracts. Robert Donald, an engineer, was elected to the Town Council in 1877 as 'Liberal and Workingman candidate'; the first organised Labour representation was obtained when two candidates were elected in 1884; six were returned to the School Board next year. The Council owed much to James C. Thompson, a moulder and later a newsagent, president 1883-85, William Johnston, blacksmith, secretary 1887-1907, who became a bailie, and George Bisset, president 1886-88, a master blacksmith, afterwards City Treasurer and chairman of the Co-operative Society.

Councils were formed for Motherwell and district in 1889, for Govan and district and for Falkirk in 1890, for Paisley in 1891 and Coatbridge in 1894; others existed by the end of the century in Arbroath, Dunfermline, Greenock, Montrose and Port Glasgow.

The idea of a federation of Scottish trade unions, partially and temporarily effected in the 'seventies, was still upheld; it was discussed abortively in 1886, and revived a decade later, when a scheme promoted by the *Clarion* found much favour. A more limited enterprise, chiefly to aid in trade disputes, was launched in October 1891, when the East of Scotland Labour Federation was formed at a conference representing 17 trades. A delegate council was appointed, and a strike levy decided upon. Edinburgh Trades Council appointed speakers to further the cause at meetings of trades, but no permanent success resulted.

Conferences on particular matters were frequent, e.g. Glasgow Trades Council held several on successive Saturdays in the summer of 1887, to consider 8-hour legislation, piecework, emigration, etc.; while in 1893 a special one on Fatal Accidents Bills took place.

The 8-hour day was a subject of chief contemporary interest, and to encourage legislative action, a Scottish Legal Eight Hours Day League was formed at a conference summoned by Glasgow Trades Council in September 1891; the ubiquitous Chisholm Robertson acted as secretary, and something of a stage army was organised.

Partly to deal with recognisably Scottish concerns, partly as a result of the extrusion of Trades Councils from direct representation at the British Trades Union Congress, a Scottish Trades Union Congress was established in March 1897. The way had been prepared by a series of delegate conferences of Trades Councils during the previous few years. No new executive authority was set up, nor were political activities envisaged; a co-ordinating body to secure the greatest common measure of agreement was contemplated. At the first congress in Glasgow, 55 organisations, with over 40,000 members, were represented by 74 delegates. Duncan McPherson of the local Trades Council presided, and the platform party included Rev. Professor (afterwards Principal Sir) G. Adam Smith and Mr. (afterwards Professor) Ronald M. Burrows. A Parliamentary Committee was formed, with Andrew Ballantyne, a civil servant, as secretary; he was soon succeeded by Miss Margaret H. Irwin, of the Council for Women's Trades. These names indicate that working-class representation was not narrowly defined. A resolution favouring collective ownership of land and capital was almost unanimously adopted. At the Congress of 1900 sharp division of opinion on the Boer War was apparent.

Some official recognition was afforded to the Scottish trade union movement by the appointment of Chisholm Robertson to the Royal Commission on Mining Royalties (1890) and of Henry Tait to that on Labour (1891), and by the invitation to trade unions and trades councils to supply evidence and data for the latter. Several prominent trade union officials were subsequently appointed official Correspondents to the Board of Trade. Scotland thus shared in the general if gradual movement towards the acceptance of trade unionism as an integral part of the British constitutional structure.

POLITICAL ACTIVITIES

National action in the political sphere was stimulated by the agitation of Keir Hardie at successive Trades Union Congresses, his candidature for Mid Lanark in April 1888, and his formation immediately afterwards of the Scottish Labour Party (May 1888). Though supported by some active trade unionists, this body had no direct connection with union organisation. Hardie indeed professed to stand primarily for 'independent working class representation', but welcomed 'peer or peasant' who would support this policy. The Party co-ordinated varied 'advanced' groups and their adherents—the Highland Land League, an outcome of a belated effort to assert crofters' rights; the Scottish Land and Labour League, which became associated with the Social Democratic Federation and its breakaway offshoot, the Socialist League, and Irish and Scottish Home Rulers. Its programme included nationalisation of banks, mines and railways, federal devolution, etc.

Tentative steps were soon taken towards more direct trade union action; these culminated in the foundation, at a conference in Edinburgh on 8th September 1891, of the Scottish United Trades Council Labour Party. The executive was to comprise representatives of Trades Councils and also of the Scottish Labour Party; the latter was soon excluded, and local organisation was based on the Trades Councils. A conference was held in Glasgow in March 1892, at which John W. Warrington of the local Trades Council presided. Chisholm Robertson was appointed secretary and a programme was adopted, advocating the 8-hour day, adult suffrage, payment of M.P.s, triennial Parliaments, local option, nationalisation of land, mines and railways.

Candidates were nominated or endorsed at the General Election of 1892, among them being John Wilson of the Shale-miners in Central Edinburgh, and Chisholm Robertson in Stirlingshire. Dundee and Greenock Councils however refused to affiliate, Edinburgh withdrew in October 1892, and though it claimed 30 branches it was dissolved at a conference in March 1893. An ineffective attempt at revival was made by Chisholm Robertson and H. H. Champion, then influential in Aberdeen, at a conference in October 1893 in Dundee.

At the very end of the century, a more lasting success was achieved by the formation at a conference in Glasgow in January 1900 of the Scottish Workers' Representation Committee. It comprised representatives from trade unions, trades councils (e.g. Glasgow), Co-operative Societies, the I.L.P. and the S.D.F. It derived much support from the beginning from the Miners; Robert Smillie was the first chairman. It was more broadly based than the contemporary Labour Representation Committee formed in London the same year, which returned two candidates—

one being Keir Hardie, for Merthyr, at the subsequent General Election.

A Housing Council for Scotland, advocating municipal enterprise, was formed in December 1900; its executive comprised trades council and co-operative representatives.

Meantime avowedly Socialist propaganda and organisation had proceeded apace, and did much to prepare the way for these developments. Its definite emergence came with the formation of Social Democratic Federation branches in Edinburgh and Glasgow in 1884; the latter resulted from a public lecture by H. M. Hyndman. Its active members included J. Bruce Glasier (1859-1920); Robert Banner, an Edinburgh bookbinder, became a member of the national executive. The Scottish Land and Labour League, formed in 1885, centred in Edinburgh; it affiliated with the S.D.F., and its secretary, John L. Mahon (1863-1900), also entered the executive. In December 1884 began the split in the S.D.F., headed by William Morris and Belfort Bax. This extended to Scotland, where the secessionists, among whom were Banner, Glasier and Mahon, set up a branch of the Socialist League in Glasgow. This existed until about 1893; the chairman for a short time was James Mavor, a university lecturer and member of a well-known business family, uncle of 'James Bridie'. He soon resigned, and became a professor in Canada; in his reminiscences, he describes the movement as 'neither indigenous to Scotland nor proletarian in composition'. The Edinburgh branch was headed by Andreas Scheu (1844-1927), an Austrian refugee; he was an architectural draughtsman, and later a commercial traveller, and was a 'consummate orator'. William Morris spoke in several Scottish towns under the auspices of the League.

The S.D.F. was kept in being in Scotland largely through the efforts of its secretary, William Nairne, a stonemason in Glasgow (d. 1901), an active propagandist and regular contributor to the official organ *Justice*. The Edinburgh branch was distinguished by the activities of James Connolly, afterwards a leader of the Dublin rising of 1916, who worked as a carter for Edinburgh Corporation and stood for the Town Council there. John Leslie, an insurance agent of Irish origin (d. 1921), though handicapped for life by an accident in boyhood, was a most energetic propagandist in Edinburgh; he was chiefly responsible for the creation of a Scottish Socialist Federation which included members of the S.D.F., Socialist League and other groups, and ultimately merged in the S.D.F. He was secretary of the local branch of the Scottish Labour Party until its absorption in the I.L.P. A Scottish District Council of the S.D.F. was formed in 1898. An S.D.F. candidate, William Cooper, was elected to Aberdeen Town Council in 1895. Study circles under its auspices expounded Marxist thought.

An Aberdeen Socialist Society, emerging from the Scottish Land and Labour League, became a branch of the S.D.F. in 1893. It is described as 'violently republican in sentiment', and demonstrated for land nationalisation and the claims of the unemployed. Its leading spirit James Leatham (1865-1945), a printer, issued for six weeks in 1891-92 a weekly *Worker's Herald*; he published many propagandist pamphlets, and was in later life editor of the *Gateway* and provost of Turriff (Aberdeenshire).

The Scottish Land Restoration League was founded in 1884, under the influence of Henry George, who toured Scotland in that year. His 'single tax' theories had been anticipated in Scotland a generation earlier by Patrick Edward Dove (1815-73), a publicist who, though of English birth, was the most active exponent of mid-century Scottish nationalism. William Forsyth, of the Cobden Hotel, Glasgow, was president of the League, whose executive included Bruce Glasier and J. Shaw Maxwell (1874-1929). At the General Election of 1885 it ran five candidates, including Morrison Davidson and Shaw Maxwell, for constituencies in the Clyde area. A monthly *Single Tax* was issued, and it later became part of the League for the Taxation of Land Values. James Cherry (d. 1900), an employee of Beardmore's, was an active exponent, and Richard McGhee, later Irish Nationalist M.P., for a time Scottish organiser. Its secretary, John Murdoch (1881-1903), a former excise officer, edited *The Highlander*, an Inverness weekly (1873-81), and wrote on *The Crofter Revolt* (1886).

The Highland Land League upheld the cause of the Scottish crofters, in whose interest Dr. Gavin Brown Clark (1840-1925), who had been associated with the First International, and another representative were elected to Parliament in 1885 and 1886, and several others to county councils after their establishment in 1889.

A Scottish Home Rule Association, of whose London branch J. Ramsay MacDonald became secretary, also came into being.

Members of these and other 'rebel' bodies, few definitely Socialist, were (as already stated) associated with the promotion of the Scottish Labour Party in May 1888. It was publicly launched at a conference in Glasgow on 25th August, with R. B. Cunninghame Graham, then a Radical M.P., as honorary president, Dr. G. B. Clark and John Ferguson, an Irish Protestant nationalist (1836-1906), a Glasgow councillor (1893-1906), as vice-presidents; J. Shaw Maxwell became chairman and Keir Hardie secretary. It was represented by Hardie at the Congress in Paris in 1889 which founded the Second International. Its fifth annual conference was held in Glasgow at New Year 1894, with Keir Hardie in the chair, and representatives of 24 branches of the Party and from over 40 trade union and co-operative bodies. Among motions approved was one demanding complete adult suffrage. At a final conference held on 26th December 1894, it was unanimously agreed to dissolve the Party and merge in the I.L.P., formed at a conference of Labour and Socialist Societies held at Bradford in January 1893. The first National Administrative Council of the I.L.P. included Hardie as chairman, Shaw Maxwell as secretary, George Carson and Chisholm Robertson.

Maltman Barry, a mysterious figure associated with the First International, exemplifying the recurrent 'Tory' strain in the Labour movement, sought to maintain relations between the Conservative Party and workers' organisations. He was the go-between with Hyndman in the 'Tory gold' episode in 1885, and was active in the early 'nineties, especially in Aberdeen. He was 'Conservative Democrat' candidate for Banffshire in 1892, advocating a legal 8-hour day and old-age pensions.

At the 1895 election, six Labour candidates stood unsuccessfully in Glasgow and district. The I.L.P. opposed the Boer War, and was associated with a 'Stop the War' movement and conciliation committee; the Scottish branch was headed by Bailie John Ferguson, with David Lowe as secretary. Riotous meetings were held in Glasgow and elsewhere, Lloyd-George being a chief speaker.

Other small groups with Socialist sympathies came into being. A 'Labour Army' formed by Frank Smith established a branch in Bridgeton, Glasgow, in 1891, with James Morton as president, and inaugurated lectures in the Albion Hall. It merged with the I.L.P., which took over the lectures. The Clarion Scouts, associated with Blatchford, were also active. The Ruskin Society, of which there were branches in several towns about 1890, propagated their master's criticisms of the social order. A few years earlier an Edinburgh University Social Reform Society, consisting chiefly of students inspired by Ruskin, pioneered the Edinburgh Social Enquiry Association (1886), officially neutral, but critical of the existing economic system. Arising therefrom, Scottish branches of the Christian Socialist Society were formed in 1887. John Warrington, the Trades Council leader, was its secretary in Glasgow. In Edinburgh, the most conspicuous figure was Rev. John Glasse (1848-1918) of Old Greyfriars Parish Church. Labour or 'People's' Churches existed for some time in Bridgeton, Glasgow (1896-98), Aberdeen (*c.* 1894) and Dundee (1892). Rev. Alexander Webster (1840-1918), who held Unitarian pastorates in several Scottish towns, was active in the Land Restoration League, and co-operated in the formation of the Scottish Labour Party. He was author of many pamphlets, and about 1888 issued a periodical, *The Ploughshare*.

Keir Hardie for a time edited *The Miner* as a Labour organ. On the foundation of the I.L.P. it gave place to the national *Labour Leader*. A Labour Literature Society, which developed into the Civic Press, was set up in Glasgow in May 1891. The *Musselburgh Monthly Reporter* was issued for a few years, from 1897, by Robert Hogg, secretary of the local I.L.P.; he emigrated to New Zealand, where he attained prominence as a Socialist journalist. Rev. James Forrest, Unitarian minister in Kilmarnock, was in 1887-88 circulating monthly letters on Christian Socialist principles to his congregation; he was afterwards lecturer under the McQuaker Trust.

The outstanding example of the Labour press was the *Glasgow Echo*. Arising from a lockout of compositors on the *Citizen* staff, a *Bulletin* was issued for 32 numbers (January to April 1893) and evolved into an evening daily, price one halfpenny. A Glasgow Newspaper Co. issued a prospectus seeking a capital of £30,000 to carry it on as an organ of 'radical and progressive principles'. The directors included the secretary of Glasgow Trades Council and several other trade union leaders. David Balsillie was appointed editor, and the first issue appeared on 8th May. Losses were reported by the middle of the next year. The periodical specialised in trade union as well as local and national news. Its editorial policy inclined to 'Lib-Lab', though it offered expression to various sections of the movement. It succumbed in September 1895. The *Aberdeen Labour Elector* (later *Aberdeen Standard*) a weekly, controlled by Champion, ran from January 1893 to February 1894. William Stewart conducted the monthly *Worker* in his native Dunfermline for a few years before joining the staff of the *Labour Leader* in 1899.

Chapter V

THE TWENTIETH CENTURY: PRE-WAR YEARS

The relatively short period from 1900 to the outbreak of war in 1914 was one of apparently renewed prosperity, apart from a set-back in 1908-10 when unemployment was serious; but rising prices precluded an increase in the purchasing power of wages. The epoch is dominated by two interrelated factors—the great advance in political action and the prevalence of large-scale industrial unrest. Both of these are phenomena common to Great Britain as a whole; this fact is in itself a main indication of the virtual economic unification of England and Scotland. From now on, it is therefore increasingly difficult to demarcate purely Scottish activities in the trade union field, and unnecessary to give so detailed an account of individual unions, though a rather indefinable influence of national characteristics may still be detected.

The process of absorption of Scottish by English unions kept pace with the absorption of Scottish by English firms. Before the century began, the Yorkshire National Union of Textile Workers had undertaken organisation in the Border woollen area, but this collapsed early in the century.

In the building trades, the Associated and the Amalgamated Carpenters and Joiners, the former of Glasgow origin, divided Scottish allegiance until their union in September 1911. The former had then over 4000 members in 129 branches, of which two were Irish and 29 English.

In the heavy industries, the Steel Smelters and the Shipwrights, though initiated in Scotland, had become predominantly English in composition, and had already transferred their headquarters south of the Border. The Blacksmiths, with a membership of about 3000 (1907), remained centred in Glasgow. The Engineers, Patternmakers, Blastfurnacemen and Boilermakers had from the start been British unions; their administration was centralised, and thus productive of friction. On the death of George Ferguson, William Brodie was elected 'Scottish organising district delegate' of the A.S.E. (1912). The Federation of Shipbuilding Trades included the Patternmakers, Ironmoulders, Blacksmiths, Joiners, Brassfinishers, Shipwrights and Boilermakers. This body negotiated with the Clyde Federated Shipbuilding Employers regarding rates of pay (January 1903). A Clyde District Committee was formed under the chairmanship of William G. Sharp (1872-1942) of the Boilermakers; he became in 1917 technical adviser of the Shipbuilders and Engineers Federation, and sat as an independent councillor for Fairfield, 1929-35.

The Associated Ironmoulders, now the doyen of Scottish unions, had about 8000 members at the commencement of their eightieth year (1910); they were then suffering from trade depression and a consequent drain on their funds for 'idle benefit'. John Brown became general secretary, in succession to J. M. Jack (December 1912).

The Scottish Electrical Union was merged in the national union in 1913, with Tom Stewart as Scottish organiser.

The Railwaymen, but for a fraction, had been absorbed in an English union (A.S.R.S.) after the strike of 1890. As a result of its coalescence with others in 1913 to form the National Union of Railwaymen, the organisation in Scotland was remodelled, under two district officers. About the same date, a North British Railway Agents Association was absorbed by the Railway Clerks' Association.

The 'new' Unions of Dockers and Sailors had spread from London to Scottish ports. A Scottish Union of Dock Labourers, with 6000-7000 members, was formed in 1911, with Joseph Houghton as secretary, and waged a successful dispute in Dundee; next year it became associated with the Transport Workers' Federation. The Seamen were reorganised early in 1906, when about 500 were enrolled in Glasgow; a national strike took place in 1911. Thereafter, in opposition to the domination of this body by Havelock Wilson, a British Seafarers' Union arose in Southampton and Glasgow, with 4000-5000 members. Emanuel Shinwell, originally a tailor, active in the Trades Council, which supported his action, formed the Glasgow branch and became national organiser (1912). It amalgamated with the National Union of Ship Stewards in 1918, and was disbanded in 1927.

The still later unions of distributive and 'black-coated' workers

—the National Union of Clerks (1890), the Shop Assistants (1891) and Railway Clerks (1897), and the various organisations of postal employees and civil servants—were from the outset constituted on a British basis. They usually had Scottish District Councils, or similar groups which met in periodic conference; e.g. the Scottish branches and national district council of the National Union of Shop Assistants, organised by John Turner, with Mary Macarthur (of whom more later) as chairman and Leslie of Portobello as secretary (1902). In January 1910 they demanded a 60-hour week and the abolition of the living-in system. In 1912, they had 28 Scottish branches. In February 1909 ten unions, including most of those catering for general and unskilled workers, agreed to mutual recognition of membership, transference and joint action in disputes.

The most important example of Scottish independence was in mining. Though participating actively in the Miners' Federation of Great Britain, of which Smillie was long president, the Scottish Federation retained a large measure of national and local autonomy; it normally had a strength of about 50,000. Protracted negotiations took place for its conversion into a national union, with responsibility for industrial disputes, while other concerns were to be left largely to county associations. A scheme was approved in principle early in 1913, but not brought into operation until the beginning of 1915.

In the shale industry of the Lothians, the underground workers, under the guidance of John Wilson, secretary of the union from its foundation until his death in 1912, drew aloof from the Scottish Miners' Federation, though formally affiliated until autumn 1922. A Joint Board of Shale Miners, Oil Workers, and Colliery Enginemen negotiated with employers.

New developments in transport stimulated the formation of the Scottish Horse and Motormen's Union. It evolved out of the Scottish Carters' Association formed in 1898 in Glasgow, which had a nominal organisation throughout Scotland, but was moribund and in debt by April 1902, when the secretary John Sampson resigned. In his place was appointed Hugh Lyon (1872-1940), an ironmoulder, formerly secretary of Falkirk Trades Council, who had been employed for about a year as district organiser. The Society was reorganised and built up considerable funds; it adopted the new title in August 1908. There was a West of

Scotland Association, with Peter Gillespie as secretary, which won a strike in Dundee in December 1911. Lyon wrote in 1919 a detailed account on the early history of his union. There was also an Edinburgh and Leith Carters' and General Workers' Union.

The most interesting advance in independent Scottish unionism was the formation in 1913 of the Scottish Farm Servants Union; it originated in Aberdeenshire but soon spread throughout Scotland. Its real founder, Joseph F. Duncan, was at its inception president of Aberdeen Trades Council, and secretary since 1903 of a local Scottish Steam Fishing Vessels Enginemen and Firemen's Union dating from 1899. He continued to hold the general secretaryship of both and acquired a unique position in not only the trade union sphere but also the public life of Scotland; he became chairman of the Landworkers' International.

The older Scottish unions which maintained their independence were chiefly in the consumptional trades—Bakers, Boot and Shoemakers, Tailors, Printers. The Bakers, of whom Thomas Reid was national secretary, had in 1910 a dispute regarding the affiliation of pastry bakers.

In the building trades, Masons, Plumbers, Plasterers, Painters and Slaters all had separate Scottish unions. The Scottish Operative Masons sustained a severe defeat in 1904, and their union was almost dormant until 1911, when it revived under the secretaryship of John F. Armour, an active Socialist propagandist. The Aberdeen society (Masons and Granite Workers), with a full-time secretary from 1895, remained independent until after the war. Of the other building unions, the Amalgamated Slaters showed most progress; in 1903 they instituted friendly benefit and appointed their first general secretary, William Cross.

In the textiles, there still existed minute local unions of specialised workers, such as the Calender Workers of Dundee, with about 1000 members, the Block Printers of Barrhead, and the Textile Workers of Newmilns. Dunfermline, a centre of the fine linen industry, had a Textile Workers' Union, formed in 1898, which enrolled about 2300 women, nearly 50 per cent of those employed. It joined with the Cloth Lappers, Powerloom Tenters and Yard Dressers in a Dunfermline and District Textile Workers' Federation, but this was disbanded in 1903. The Powerloom Tenters survived to wage a strike in autumn 1907, when blacklegs were expelled. A Scottish Federation of Powerloom Tenters was founded in January 1908, with John Burt as secretary; it amalgamated with an English union in 1911. A Fife Cloth Lappers and Finishers' Association existed in 1905. A Joint Committee of Textile Workers, apparently for this area, was formed in May 1913 and held a successful campaign for shorter hours.

The Dundee Mill and Factory Operatives Union of 1885, in which Rev. Henry Williamson remained the leading figure, virtually collapsed through an unsuccessful strike in March 1903. In its place the Dundee and District Union of Jute and Flax Workers was organised, with the aid of Mary Macarthur, in March 1906. John F. Syme (d. 1943) was secretary until 1940. By 1912 it had 12,000 members and funds of about £1000. It was four-fifths feminine in composition and reserved half of the seats on its executive for women. The Scottish Mill Factory and Bleachfield Workers' Federation (1887) operating mainly in Angus, claimed about 2000 in 1911. Between them, these unions organised less than half of the workers eligible, and were handicapped by the diversity of pay and conditions, the irresponsibility and indiscipline of their members, and the unwillingness of employers to accord recognition. A Kirkcaldy Dressers' Union, disrupted by a strike, in 1912 proposed to affiliate to the Federation.

A Scottish Textile Trades Federation was formed in 1909, on the initiative of the warpers; it combined women weavers with some of the more specialised male craft workers.

The National Union of Dyers, a Yorkshire union, organised workers in the Vale of Leven in 1911 and conducted a successful strike in December.

Several local textile societies were affiliated to the Women's Trade Union League (1874). The National Federation of Women Workers was established in England in 1906 as a general union, with the already mentioned Mary Macarthur (1880-1921, afterwards Mrs. W. C. Anderson), a native of Ayr, as secretary. With the support of Edinburgh Trades Council, this union formed a branch of about 500, during a strike in a paper box factory (1907), and organised women in the dyeworks in conjunction with the National Union of Dyers (1911). An Aberdeen Union of Women Workers was formed in 1909 with the Marchioness of Aberdeen as president. The laboriously organised women's unions in the West had collapsed. The Scottish Council for Women's Trades held a national conference in Glasgow in October 1907 and an exhibition of sweated industries in Glasgow in March 1913, in connection with the agitation for Trades Boards. It continued affiliation with the Trades Union Congress; a motion for its expulsion was defeated by a two-to-one majority in 1913.

The first decade of the century was relatively peaceful, though in the autumn of 1908 the prevalence of unemployment occasioned demonstrations and disturbances in Glasgow. Cunninghame Graham then made his last appearance as a Labour agitator, and advocated the construction of a motor track to Edinburgh as a form of public employment for the workless. A Glasgow District Unemployed Workers' Committee, formed in 1906, on which J. F. Armour, organiser of the S.D.F., A. R. Turner, organiser of the Municipal Employees' Association, and Thomas A. Kerr of the I.L.P., were active, carried on a 'Right to Work' propaganda among trade unions and the Labour Party. A conference of about 200 delegates in June 1908 sought the formation of similar committees throughout Scotland, and arranged a public demonstration. At another conference in January 1910, the name was altered to 'The Right to Work Committee'; Glasgow Trades Council became represented on it, and the Scottish Trades Union Congress in April endorsed the demand for 'work or maintenance'.

In the years immediately prior to the war of 1914 there were large-scale industrial conflicts, in which Scotland was involved. These commenced with a lockout of shipyard workers, including about 6000 on the Clyde (May 1908), and a national lockout of boilermakers, arising partly from a dispute at Partick (September to December 1910). A notable episode was the national strike of seamen and dockers in the summer of 1911, directed by the newly formed Transport Workers' Federation. It was followed by local dockers' disputes in Dundee in December 1911 and Glasgow early in 1912. The national railway strike of 1911 led in 1913 to the amalgamation of several unions in the National Union of Railwaymen (1913). A Clyde District Workers' Joint Committee, representative of Dockers, Seamen, Motormen, etc., was in existence in December 1911.

These struggles were put in the shade by the miners' strike of 1912, the largest that had ever occurred in Great Britain, involving a million men; it was terminated by the passing of the Minimum Wage Act. A primarily Scottish dispute arose in 1914, when the local unions reverted to the policy of 'restricted darg' (a 4-day week), but were refused support by the Miners' Federation of Great Britain. The dispute was unsettled at the outbreak of war, as was a builders' strike.

Among disputes of more localised scope were Edinburgh tramway strikes of August 1903 and July 1913, and an involved controversy in the Edinburgh printing trades. In November 1909, the Edinburgh Typographical Society presented a memorandum to the employers asking that there should be no further increase in the number (then about 5000) of women employed, some of whom were organised in the Amalgamated Society of Warehousemen. Several abortive conferences were held, though some firms sympathised with the demand. A strike was called in September 1910, but within a fortnight a compromise was reached, postponing for six years the further admission of women. A recently formed Edinburgh Women Compositors, Readers and Monotype Operators' Union opposed the strike. Permanent exclusion of women from certain skilled jobs continued, and apprenticeship remained strictly limited, so that the craft remained one of the closest in the country. The Typographical Society, with four others, affiliated to the Printing and Kindred Trades' Association.

Trades Councils grew in numbers; e.g. two were formed in Fife—Kirkcaldy (1912) and Methil (1912). They tended to become more politically minded, perhaps at the expense of industrial organisation. In 1903, Glasgow Trades Council comprised 255 delegates, representing 70,000 members of 243 organisations. A disastrous fire at the Albion Hall, Glasgow, the meeting place of the Trades Council and of many local unions, destroyed much of their records and other property, including a Trades Council Reference Library, with rare books and pamphlets (August 1909). Labour Day demonstrations were held on the first Sunday in May. Edinburgh Trades Council arranged a District Committee for unions outwith the city; this covered thirteen unions with about 15,000 members, and met monthly. The Council also assisted in the successful strike of tramwaymen in municipal employment.

The Scottish Trades Union Congress met annually in spring,

and shared with Glasgow Trades Council the services of George Carson (1848-1921) as secretary. It was much divided on the issue of secular education, which it favoured at successive conferences from 1906; Catholic trade unionists, including the miners' leaders, Doonan, Murnin, Sullivan and Tonner, demonstrated against the project in 1909. In 1908 a resolution for the prohibition of alcoholic liquor was carried by a majority of one, but normally municipalisation of its sale was preferred. Compulsory arbitration was rejected by a three-to-one majority, and a Right to Work Bill unanimously approved. In 1911 Congress adopted a Charter to be awarded to approved trade unions and trades councils.

POLITICAL ACTIVITIES

In the political sphere, the Scottish Workers' Representation Committee, established in January 1900, held annual conferences, usually presided over by Henry Murphy (d. June 1912), chairman of Lanark Co-operative Society, director of S.C.W.S. and member of the I.L.P. A proposal in 1903 for co-ordination with the English body was at the time ineffective. In the 1906 election, two nominees of the latter, Alexander Wilkie in Dundee and George N. Barnes in Glasgow, both secretaries of large national unions, were elected, against Liberal and Conservative opponents. The Scottish Committee sponsored five unsuccessful candidates, all miners, in three-cornered contests.

The Committee now designated itself the Scottish Labour Party and set up some local machinery. There was recurrent friction with the national body, to which it affiliated in 1908; and at the ninth annual conference, in January 1909, a resolution merging it in the larger unit, known since 1906 as the Labour Party, was carried by 81 to 36. In 1913 a Scottish Advisory Council of the Labour Party was established, with an annual conference and full-time secretary; this office was long held by Ben Shaw.

Nine Scottish seats were unsuccessfully fought by the Labour Party in the election of January 1910, and three in that of December. Barnes and Wilkie retained their seats on both occasions, with Liberal support, and were joined on the latter by William Adamson, secretary of the Fife Miners, who captured the West Fife division from a Liberal. After 1910 the Parliamentary group acquired a disproportionate importance owing to the virtual equality of the two chief parties; along with the Irish Nationalists, Labour held the balance, which was generally swayed in favour of the Liberal Government as long as the contest with the House of Lords endured. Their support was rewarded by the measure repealing the Osborne Judgment, and thus legalising the exaction by trade unions of contributions to a political fund. An interdict had meantime been taken out against the Scottish Typographical Association.

In municipal representation there was a marked advance. In Edinburgh and Leith, where many unsuccessful contests had been waged under varied auspices, the Workers Municipal Committee, chiefly of trade union composition, formed in 1899, ran candidates for the Town and Parish Councils and School Board, but few were successful; one nominee was elected to the Town Council in 1900. Nominally, political action was administered separately from September 1905 to April 1920; a local section of the Scottish Workers' Representation Committee was set up at the former date, and converted into the Edinburgh branch of the Labour Party in April 1907. The first official Labour Councillor was returned in 1909, and at the outbreak of war the Party had six representatives on the Town Council, four on the Parish Council and two on the School Board.

Glasgow had continuous Labour representation from 1889, on the whole increasing. A Workers' Municipal Election Committee, with representatives from the Trades Council, trade unions, I.L.P., Co-operatives, and Irish National League set up in 1895, with Joseph Burgess as secretary was reconstituted in March 1904. In the years just before the war, councillors rose rapidly to 17; at a 'general' election, due to extension of boundaries, in 1912, four new members were elected, including John Wheatley. The local Labour Party formed a Housing Committee which held annual conferences.

A local periodical, the *Scottish Labour Observer*, ran for about a year in Paisley (1905-06). A great advance in Labour journalism was made with the commencement of *Forward* in Glasgow on 13th October 1906, under the editorship of Thomas Johnston. Published weekly, and chiefly propagandist in matter, it was from the start, independent of official control, being privately financed. It was printed by the Glasgow Civic Press.

Jesus in Juteopolis (1906), by Walter Walsh, long minister of an independent church in Dundee, and *Allanforth Commune* (1913) by Findlay Watt, were Scottish examples of the didactic fiction, with a Socialist moral, then popular.

The I.L.P. was the most active propagandist body in Scotland, which was one of its strongholds. A Dunfermline Socialist Society, formed in 1900, affiliated to it in 1906. A Scottish Council was formed in 1906, and this became one of the Divisional Councils into which the national organisation was divided; George Kerr (1906-09; d. 1942), George Dallas (1910-12) and William Stewart (1912-33; d. 1947), a former linen factory worker of literary gifts, contributor to *Forward* and biographer of Keir Hardie, were successively secretary. There were about fifty Scottish branches. The annual national conference was held in Edinburgh in 1909; there were then five branches in that city. The 'Reformers' Bookstall' was established in Glasgow in 1907 in connection with the I.L.P., managed by Hardie's brother David. James Maxton, school teacher, and Patrick Dollan, of Irish descent, at first a miner, were among its best known propagandists in the pre-war years; the activities of these and other I.L.P. leaders are described in *Clydesiders* (1965) by R. K. Middlemas.

The Social Democratic Federation, which had a branch in Glasgow from 1884, formed a Scottish District Council in 1898, and expanded after the Boer War. Thomas Kennedy was appointed full-time organiser in 1903, and by 1910 there were 40 branches. James Burnett, a railway signalman, was district secretary, and John Maclean (1879-1923), a teacher under Govan School Board, became a prominent spokesman. The S.D.F. seceded from the Workers' Representation Committee after its first year; it was absorbed in the British Socialist Party founded in October 1911, and just prior to the war the new body sought affiliation to the Labour Party.

The Socialist Labour Party arose from a Glasgow secession from the S.D.F. in 1903; James Connolly became organiser, and Neil McLean, afterwards Labour M.P., its first secretary. It published the *Socialist* and conducted classes in Marxist economics, led by a draughtsman, George Yates, and Thomas Bell, an ironmoulder, whose *Pioneering Days* is a chief source of information. The Socialist Party of Great Britain (1904) was another fraction centred in Glasgow.

Local Fabian Societies existed sporadically during this period in the principal towns and the universities. In Glasgow these were for some years strong; the Edinburgh City Society had a continuous existence from about 1910, with D. B. Mackay as secretary.

The Socialist Sunday School movement survived the Labour churches with which it had been associated, and attained some prominence, especially on Clydeside.

Chamberlain's Tariff Reform campaign sought trade union support; a Trade Union Tariff Reform Association formed an Edinburgh branch in August 1906, with Alexander Boag, of Leith Operative Tailors, as chairman. Professor J. Robertson Watson of Glasgow Technical College, an early Labour adherent, a candidate in 1895, became a leading supporter. Glasgow Trades Council, after prolonged debate, passed a resolution against food taxes and in favour of a land tax (December 1903).

The growth of social consciousness in the Church was indicated, e.g. by a Labour Week, held by Glasgow United Free Presbytery in April 1911, in which the Moderator of the Presbytery and the trade union leaders William Adamson and John Hodge took part; and by the lectures and books of Rev. Dr. Wilson Harper and Rev. Dr. John Glasse. The kinship between Irish nationalism and the Scottish 'rebel' movement, already noticeable in the Chartist period and the Home Rule crisis, revived, and was fostered by the Catholic Socialist Society, formed in 1906 by John Wheatley (1869-1930), of Irish immigrant stock, originally a miner, who established a printing business and became a local councillor.

Movements for working-class education were set afoot in this period. A very representative conference of 364 delegates, held in St. Andrew's Hall, Glasgow, on 16th October 1909, initiated the Workers' Educational Association in Scotland; Principal Macalister of Glasgow University presided, and F. W. Jowett, M.P., and R. H. Tawney were chief speakers. A provisional committee was set up, including six representatives each of trade unions, friendly societies, co-operatives, socialist societies and other groups. A Glasgow branch had as secretary Robert Small, Scottish Organiser of the General Federation of Trade Unions.

A branch was formed in Edinburgh in 1912, and in Aberdeen in 1913, but up to the outbreak of war the Association had not taken deep root.

Classes in Marxian economics were conducted in Glasgow from about 1907 by John Maclean, and were commenced, under the auspices of the recently founded Central Labour College, in Edinburgh in 1912.

CHAPTER VI

THE FIRST WORLD WAR AND THE INTER-WAR PERIOD

FOR Scottish trade unionism, as for other factors in the economic life of Britain, the war stimulated and intensified tendencies already apparent. It gave the Clyde area in particular a perhaps adventitious notoriety, because of the sensational episodes which occurred there.

The growth of syndicalism and a reaction against bureaucratic centralisation and the apparently compromising policy of the political movement were already manifest at the outset of the war. The war, with its demand for increased output, led to the suspension of trade union rules (which was officially accepted) and to the influx of female and other unskilled labour; it also enhanced prices and worsened the already acute shortage of adequate housing accommodation. The heavy industry of the Clyde made it a crucial centre for munitions. Here arose the first of a series of industrial disputes, through the refusal of a wage increase in engineering for which a demand was pending at the outbreak of war. A refusal to work overtime (January 1915) was followed by a strike of a fortnight's duration, led, against the desire of the trade union officials, by a Central Withdrawal of Labour Committee of shop stewards, with William Gallacher as chairman and J. M. Messer as secretary. The increase was granted as a war bonus by the Committee on Production set up by the Government. A minor dispute at Fairfield (September 1915) led to the fining under the Munition Act of several shipwrights, of whom three were imprisoned on refusal to pay. A general strike was threatened to release them, but eventually their fines were paid by their union.

A Committee of Two was sent by the Government to investigate conditions on the Clyde, and some of its recommendations were subsequently adopted. A dilution campaign was inaugurated, and resulted in the famous visit of Lloyd George as Minister of Munitions (December 1915), and the demand for workers' control of its administration. A Dilution Committee was set up in January 1916, providing for full consultation with workers' representatives. Meantime the Withdrawal of Labour Committee evolved into the Clyde Workers' Committee, with Gallacher as chairman, which organised local committees throughout the area, and from January 1916 issued the *Worker*, edited by John W. Muir. Dissatisfaction with the Munitions Act and the operation of dilution led to a strike at Beardmore's, Parkhead, in March 1916, as a result of which six leading shop stewards, including David Kirkwood and Arthur McManus, were deported from Glasgow under the Defence of the Realm Act. The Associated Iron-moulders had a Central Emergency Committee, in which Tom Bell was a chief figure; it carried on a strike in the autumn of 1917.

The Russian Revolution was followed by the Leeds Convention of June 1917, which proposed the formation of Workers' and Soldiers' Councils throughout the country. One such was formed for the Clyde area, but exercised no great influence. From a trade union point of view, perhaps the feature of most importance in these episodes (described from varied standpoints in the reminiscences of such participants as Gallacher and Kirkwood) was the role assumed by the shop stewards, especially in engineering, as a result of wartime conditions of production.

The chronic unrest on the Clyde culminated shortly after the Armistice in the Forty Hours' Strike of January 1919, to enforce a demand thrice approved by conferences held during the war, and reiterated at a special trade union conference in the last days of December. A claim forwarded in October to the Ministry of Labour had been ignored. The strike was precipitated by the general introduction of a 47-hour week in local works, since this was regarded as intended to queer the pitch for the more drastic reduction. The initiative was taken by a Ways and Means Committee appointed at a meeting of shop stewards on 5th January 1919; a manifesto was issued and work gate meetings arranged. A delegate conference of about 500 was held on 18th January; the Trades Council and the trade unions concerned were officially represented; a committee to conduct the strike was appointed, with Emanuel Shinwell (chairman of Trades Council) as chairman, and William Shaw, secretary of Trades Council, joint secretary with David Morton, a shop steward (who later published a narrative of the strike); William Gallacher became organiser. The strike commenced on 27th January, and was very complete; mass picketing was successfully employed, and elaborate organisation for this and for other purposes—e.g. relief, entertainment—was established. A national conference was held on the 28th, and a *Strike Bulletin* was issued, with a circulation of 20,000.

Large numbers of troops were imported, and a threatened sympathetic strike of electricity workers declared illegal. A march to the Municipal Buildings in George Square on 31st January was met by a police baton charge and the reading of the Riot Act. Several leaders were arrested, some injured; all except Gallacher and Shinwell were acquitted. Meantime the strike was called off on 12th February, largely because the national unions withheld support.

The cessation of the wartime demand for munitions destroyed the economic basis of the movement, and its leaders, influenced by the Russian Revolution, devoted themselves to the political sphere. The Clyde had however attained a reputation for 'redness', confirmed by the General Election of 1922. The strikes of the immediate post-war period—coal, rail, engineering, etc.—and the National Strike of 1926 affected Scotland in common with the rest of Britain, but displayed no distinctive features. The chairman and secretary of the Scottish T.U.C. took part in the conference which called the strike, and arranged to apply the general plan in Scotland. Some Scottish centres claimed to be among those most effectively and solidly organised by local strike committees, and several 'Bulletins' were published, e.g. in Edinburgh (5th to 8th May). Seventy thousand copies in six editions of a *Scottish Worker* were distributed as an official organ. Arising from the strike, a boycott of the anti-union press, especially in Dundee (Thomson-Leng combine), was maintained for several years by the printing unions, with the endorsement of the Scottish T.U.C. Some agitation was carried on, in the form of area conferences, against the Trades Disputes Act of 1927.

These and other activities of the period must be viewed against the background of the 'Great Depression' which settled on the country towards the end of 1920. In this the Clyde, because of its peculiar dependence on the export of its heavy industry products to declining foreign markets, and of their artificial expansion for war purposes, suffered with special persistence and severity, so that it was eventually scheduled as a 'special area'. Other parts of Scotland, such as Leith with its docks and Dundee with its jute manufacture, sustained similar prolonged slumps. Trade union membership and organisation accordingly fell away.

The war speeded up the process of amalgamation. In December 1916 the Associated Iron and Steel Workers, the National Steel-workers' Association and the British Steel Smelters' Association adopted a scheme by which was formed a new central association, the British Iron Steel and Kindred Trades Association, into which, to obviate legal difficulties, all new members were to be enrolled. Several other unions connected with the industry followed suit, and the Iron and Steel Trades Confederation was constituted as an interim consolidation in 1917. Scotland became a division, in charge of an 'officer'. The Confederation took the initiative in a new scheme for adult education through the Workers' Educational Association, by which facilities were accorded to members as a union 'benefit'. Scotland was one of two divisions for which a tutor-organiser was appointed. This office was discontinued in the economic crisis of 1931, the union funds having suffered severely in the depression. In February 1919 also, an agreement for 8-hour shifts, instead of 12, was reached, to be operated in Scotland by a district committee; elaborate adjustments of basic rates of pay were adopted. A reintroduction of longer shifts was enforced in 1929, a strike, the first for many years in the industry, proving unavailing.

Other amalgamations which affected Scottish unionism were those by which were founded the Amalgamated Engineering Union (1920), the National Union of General and Municipal Workers (1924) and the Transport and General Workers' Union (1922). One result was that the two General Workers' Unions came to share the textile workers of the Borders. The T.G.W.U. after two abortive efforts, absorbed the Scottish Union of Dock Labourers (1923); and in accordance with special arrangements which preserved a measure of autonomy (including separate representation at the T.U.C.) the Scottish Farm Servants' Union in 1933, and the Scottish Sea Fishers' Union in 1937. The venerable Associated Ironmoulders of Scotland, after a century of independent existence, linked up in June 1920 with the still older English society in the National Union of Foundry Workers; a National Federation of (12) Foundry Trades existed from

February 1918, and a wider union was established in 1946; the Amalgamated Union of Foundry Workers, which also embraced the Central Ironmoulders' Association, the Scottish Brassmoulders' Union, and the Associated Iron, Steel and Brass Dressers of Scotland. John McBain (1882-1941) was Scottish organiser and Hugh Murdoch (d. November 1946) and Archibald Logan other leading figures.

Long-standing strife between English and Scottish Tailors' unions was ended by their amalgamation in 1919. The Scottish Foremen's Association linked up with the Amalgamated Managers' and Foremen's Association. The Carpenters, united since 1911, absorbed the Scottish Cabinetmakers in 1918, and were merged in the Amalgamated Society of Woodworkers in January 1921.

The building trades were the scene of two purely Scottish combinations: in 1919 the Scottish Operative Masons and the Aberdeen Granite Workers formed the Building and Monumental Workers' Association of Scotland; next year the Operative Plumbers and Domestic Engineers' Association swallowed the Plumbers and the Heating Engineers.

Protracted negotiations for amalgamation of the various unions of textile workers, initiated by the T.U.C. in December 1928, and participated in by fourteen of the twenty-three unions affected, finally broke down in September 1931. The Scottish Lace and Textile Workers' Union co-ordinated all workers in the industry in Ayrshire.

Conversely, a split took place among the miners, whose eight county associations had since 6th January 1915 become more closely associated in the Scottish Mineworkers' Union, with some 100,000 members, all levied 6d. per week. The Scottish Shale Miners' Association, dating from 1886, disaffiliated in autumn 1922, and from the beginning of 1924 was incorporated with the Scottish Oilworkers' Association, established in 1900, in the National Union of Shale Miners and Oil Workers. The industry was now monopolised under Scottish Oils Ltd., which became a subsidiary of the Anglo-Persian Oil Co. Its economic position steadily deteriorated, and about one-third of its works were closed by 1926. Apart from a short strike in that year, relations with employers remained peaceful.

In 1922, a 'Reform Union' was set up in Fife by extremists, headed by Philip Hodge, an agent who had been suspended. This body published a periodical, *The Miner*; it was re-absorbed in 1927. A Lanarkshire Miners' Industrial Union was also formed as a left-wing body. As a result of further dissension, the United Mineworkers of Scotland was formed in 1929, finding its nucleus in the old Fife union, which had been disaffiliated from the National Union, and in other sections expelled from the latter; William Allan, formerly of the Lanarkshire Union, became secretary. It was disbanded in December 1935, in the interests of solidarity.

A secession also took place from the Transport and General Workers' Union. Glasgow Dockers in January 1932 formed the Scottish Transport and General Workers' Union, with nearly 4000 members. This evolved from an Anti-Registration League, which repeatedly rejected the officially accepted scheme of registration of dockers, with a view to decasualising labour. The same attitude was adopted by the Aberdeen branch of the T.G.W.U.; both adhered to an agreement of 1922 with the employers, which gave priority of engagement to unionists, and adopted restriction of membership. A government Board of Inquiry on Port Labour examined the position in 1937, and advocated a Joint Committee to operate in the main the existing system.

A Scottish Busmen's Union was also formed about 1933 by seceders from the T.G.W.U., and a number of bus employees subsequently transferred their allegiance to the Scottish Horse and Motormen's Union. These schisms, and unofficial strikes, which occurred more than once, were not so much manifestations of renascent nationalism as protests against over-centralisation and neglect of local and sectional interests in so large and heterogeneous an organisation.

The National Sailors' and Firemen's Union, which had seceded from the earlier Transport Workers Federation, sustained a further Scottish breakaway in 1921, when the National Maritime Union was founded, with branches in Glasgow and elsewhere. At the same time the British Seafarers' Union joined with the National Union of Ship Stewards to form the Amalgamated Marine Workers' Union, in close co-operation with the T.G.W.U.

Among the few new ventures may be mentioned the formation in July 1917 of a National Laundry Workers' Union; J. H. Moore, sometime Edinburgh town councillor, was national organiser, and Miss Grace Donaldson acted as honorary general secretary in Edinburgh until October 1925.

The most notable step in the organisation of black-coated workers was the formation of the Scottish Bankers' Association. This was persistently denied recognition by the Scottish banks; an attempted strike in the spring of 1937 proved a fiasco. The Union Bank was the most obdurate opponent, and dismissed an employee for his activities on the executive of the Association. A. B. Mackay, then on the staff of Glasgow Savings Bank, afterwards a town councillor, was the leading spirit. The Insurance Guild also became active in Scotland in the 1930's, when a campaign was instituted by these and allied unions of professional workers.

The National Union of Clerks (N.U.C.) formed a Scottish Council in 1915; Robert Scoullar of Greenock became secretary, and Stewart Reid was appointed organiser two years later.

The Union of Postal Workers, an amalgamation of several unions, established a Scottish Council in 1919; this held annual meetings, but relied on voluntary office-bearers. The union had to sever its active connection with the trade union movement owing to the Act of 1927. It was one of the chief supporters of the Workers' Educational Trade Union Committee. Its Glasgow branch published a monthly organ, *St. Mungo*, containing much material of general interest; it reached a high editorial standard under the direction (1922-39) of W. D. Thomson.

Of 227 unions operating in Scotland in 1924, with a total membership of 536,432, 86 had a membership of less than 100, and 75 of over 1000. Ninety of these were purely Scottish unions, with a membership of 213,469. In 1938, affiliations to the Scottish T.U.C. represented 350,000 workers, and included 40 Trades Councils.

THE SCOTTISH TRADES UNION CONGRESS

An outstanding feature of the inter-war period is the enhancement in the power and prestige of the Scottish T.U.C. The Congress, at a special conference in December 1922, followed the lead of the British body by establishing a General Council; unions were grouped in eleven sections, each of which nominated candidates, who were elected by Congress as a whole. A permanent secretaryship was instituted, and held by William Elger of the N.U.C., whose outstanding ability was a material asset in the advance of the Council's authority. The regular issue of a monthly *Bulletin* (a four-page leaflet) began in September 1926. The group system was abandoned in 1931; henceforth groups not represented on the Council were entitled to appoint representatives to advise it.

A review of the main proceedings of Congress illustrates the chief preoccupations of Scottish trade unionism during this period.

War policy and peace aims.—Organised trade unionism in general gave enthusiastic support to the war of 1914-18, but a critical attitude developed in the later years, especially on the Clyde. This is indicated by a conference in March 1917, organised by the Scottish T.U.C. and the Scottish Advisory Council of the Labour Party, which rejected compulsory industrial service, and passed an amendment, moved by James Maxton on behalf of the I.L.P., in preference to the official resolution making its acceptance contingent on the conscription of wealth. Industrial conscription was rejected also at a conference under the auspices of the National Council for Civil Liberties, held with much trade union support in Glasgow about the same date; an event notorious because of an attempt to break it up by the Scottish Patriotic Federation which led to a serious fracas. The Scottish T.U.C. a month later, while it 'cordially received' an address by Neville Chamberlain as Minister of National Service, rejected industrial conscription, demanded conscription of wealth and peace negotiations, protested against D.O.R.A.[1] and deportations, and supported state purchase of the liquor trade by 60 votes against 19 for Prohibition, advocated by Glasgow Trades and Labour Council.

The Congress of 1918 demanded a declaration of war aims by the Government, Scottish representation at the Peace Conference; approved the project of a League of Nations, and resolved in favour of socialisation of food supplies and large-scale educational reform. A special two-day conference was held after the Armistice to consider the immediate post-war situation. It demanded a 40-hour week, universal unemployment insurance, interest-free building, retention of Rent Restriction Acts, repeal of conscrip-

[1] D.O.R.A. Defence of the Realm Acts (to come).

tion and D.O.R.A., and release of conscientious objectors (27th to 28th December 1918).

Trade union organisation.—The Congress of 1924 instructed the General Council to 'make a survey of the extent and structure of the trade union movement in Scotland and to report'. The report, presented next year, and based on admittedly imperfect data, implied that only one wage-earner in three of those eligible was organised, i.e. fully half a million; fourth-fifths of the total were in 36 unions; the Lothians showed the highest percentage of membership. Congress remitted to the Council 'the preparation of a plan for developing and co-ordinating the organising activities of the unions with a view to increasing the strength of the movement'. After a series of conferences with trade union delegates, the Council circulated a 'Report on Organisation', which was approved by the 1926 conference by 134 votes to 57. The scheme provided for local and county Trade Union Committees, with functions 'which arise naturally out of the experience of trade unions in dealing with problems of organisation—Structure, Co-ordination, Non-Unionism—problems which can only be faced by the purely industrial organisation'. After the General Strike, Trades and Labour Councils were circularised, asking the appointment of special committees to co-operate. Such committees were formed in eighteen areas, but were mostly short-lived; that in Aberdeen functioned continuously and successfully. A further report was submitted to the 1938 Congress; it reaffirmed previous findings.

Special attention was given to the organisation of women. A Special Advisory Committee was set up by the 1926 Congress, and a conference of delegates from 31 unions which had women among their members was held in September 1926. About 40,000 women were members of affiliated, and about 20,000 of non-affiliated unions. A questionnaire on the position of women in unions was circulated. Conferences of unions catering for women were held annually thereafter, with a growing percentage of women delegates. Women's trade union groups were formed in some centres, and propaganda among women workers was carried on regularly.

In 1933 a special campaign was initiated to interest youth in trade unions. The 1936 Congress proposed the formation of Trade Union Fellowships under Trades Council auspices. The

General Council, after consulting Trades Councils, reported to the next Congress against a general scheme, but proposed a model constitution for use where desired; a Youth Advisory Committee and a special conference were suggested. The conference was held in September 1938, and approved these recommendations.

Local joint organisation.—During and after the war, it became usual for Trades Councils and Burgh Labour Parties to be combined in some such form as a Trades and Labour Council. This involved considerable confusion of political and industrial activities, and some dislocation of the work of the council by the prevalence of partisan conflict, especially in Glasgow. Here an Industrial Advisory Council was formed, among local trade union officials; it arranged monthly discussion meetings on topical issues (*c.* 1928). Suggestions for disjunction were frequently considered; finally, in the 1934 Congress, the General Council was instructed to investigate and report on local joint trade union bodies.

Experiments in County Trades Councils in chiefly rural areas, and in local trade union groups were attempted. In October 1938 a conference of representatives of 24 trades councils approved the separation of industrial and political sections (already agreed to by the Scottish Labour Party Conference in May), and outlined a statement as to composition, functions, policy, etc. of trades councils, which was circulated by the General Council the next month.

Wages and working conditions.—The 1926 Congress carried unanimously a resolution instructing the General Council to investigate and report on methods of regulating wages and working conditions. A preliminary report was presented next year, and was supplemented by further reports to the next two congresses, based on questionnaires. These indicated that opinions were divided as to the effect of Trades Boards and Joint Industrial Councils, and raised the issue of the statutory regulation of wages. The final report affirmed that 'legislation of wages should follow and not precede the initiative of the Unions in wages questions', and proposed 'New Statutory Machinery for Promotion of Collective Agreements' in industries where no collective bargaining existed. This should include a permanent Conciliation Officer and Board, empowered on the application of a trade union in a dispute to consider and recommend, but not to make a binding decision. These findings were adopted by a large majority in the 1930 Congress. The scheme was, with minor amendments, approved by a joint committee of the Scottish and British T.U.C., and submitted to the Minister of Labour. A memorandum was circulated to affiliated unions, and elicited varied opinions.

Fair wages clause.—A demand that the Fair Wages Clause should apply to all workers and business transactions of public bodies was unanimously passed (1931), and an inquiry subsequently made showed that this was already operative in a majority of cases. A Model Fair Wages Clause was now drafted and submitted.

The Congress of 1934 passed a resolution to ensure the employment of trade union labour by co-operative societies and their contractors. A joint committee was set up between the General Council and the Scottish Sectional Board, which issued a questionnaire to co-operative societies. This showed that trade union labour was general. It was recommended that trade unionists should become co-op. members. and that co-operative societies should adopt the Fair Wages Clause.

Demarcation disputes.—Much of the time of the Council was devoted during the period to attempts to settle disputes between unions, and these occasionally gave rise to acrimonious controversy in Congress. That of 1931 re-affirmed the powers of adjudication conferred on the Council by standing orders, which gave it no authority to lay down general principles. Affiliation was refused to several unions on the ground of their being secessionist or schismatic. In 1938 the Council was instructed to inquire into and define the appropriate union for recognition.

Unemployment.—The serious recurrence of unemployment owing to the world crisis of 1929-31 evoked action in various ways. The 1932 Congress affirmed the necessity of retaining unemployed in membership. An inquiry instituted thereupon by the Council revealed that out of 85 unions, 61, representing 70 per cent of membership, maintained the membership of unemployed at no, or at a nominal subscription, with admittedly beneficial results in a majority of cases. Many unemployed were non-unionist. The T.U.C. after conference with Trades Council representatives then formulated a scheme for local Associations of Unemployed, under Trades Council auspices, and laid down model rules. Six such Associations were formed forthwith (1933), but most projects failed.

Against some left-wing opposition, Congress endorsed acceptance by the General Council of representation on the Scottish Council for Community Service during Unemployment (December 1932). This body agreed to insist on principles advocated by the S.T.U.C., e.g. banning the sale to the public of goods made in Community Centres, and repudiating supersession of trade union aid to applicants for unemployment benefit.

The institution of the Unemployment Assistance Board also stimulated agitation against the household means test. Its abolition was called for by a conference of Trades Councils in September 1935; this was endorsed by the General Council in December.

The Congress of 1936 approved the principle of trade union co-operation on the Economic Committee of the Scottish Development Council.

'Minority' and kindred movements.—Throughout the period, the movement generally was affected by the activities of sections alleged to be under Communist influence, which under various titles came into conflict with official policy. In September 1928 the Council intimated that it rejected the affiliation of Trades Councils associated with the National Minority Movement. In February 1935 a further statement, approved by Congress in that year, was issued, insisting on conformity to T.U.C. policy by affiliated organisations. An approach by the National Unemployed Workers' Movement was rejected (January 1936). As in England, this body, of which Scotland constituted a district, had organised the unemployed independently of official trade union machinery. Persistent demonstrations in support of demands for abolition of the means test, increased children's allowances, reduction of rents, etc., culminated in a 'Scottish Hunger March' to Edinburgh, to interview the Secretary for Scotland (June 1933). Some of the marchers encamped and fed on the main streets of the city; ultimately the Corporation provided transport for their return home. An earlier march (December 1922) on London had included a Scottish contingent under the leadership of the 72-year-old James Morton.

Education and research.—The T.U.C. continued affiliation to both N.C.L.C. and W.E.A. until 1936, when support of the latter was refused by a majority of five. By a majority of four, the same Congress declined an offer of representation on the governing board of the newly founded Newbattle Abbey Adult Education College, although the General Council had been represented on a provisional committee which drew up its constitution.

A resolution proposing the establishment of a research department was carried in 1935, but the Council found its creation impracticable, while prepared to carry on periodic research into problems as they arose.

International situation.—Congress associated itself with the official policy of the Labour Party, especially in respect of collective security. The triumph of Nazism directed its attention particularly to foreign affairs, especially in view of the hostility of the new German regime to trade unionism. Internal differences of Right and Left were rather with regard to method than to principle, proposals for United and Popular Fronts being disavowed. A manifesto supporting the war was issued at its outbreak in September 1939, and approved by Congress in April 1940. Disaffiliation from the Scottish Peace Council was approved, and a capital levy was unanimously demanded.

The developments referred to above necessitated some change in the form and activities of Trades Councils. In April 1918 the Glasgow Trades Council was reconstituted, by a vote of delegate conferences, as Glasgow Trades and Labour Council; the Glasgow Labour Party and Govan Trades Council were absorbed. Owing to legal difficulties, special arrangements were made for the affiliation of Co-operative Societies. A Local Labour Party was formed in each Parliamentary constituency. There were about 350 affiliated organisations, representing over 100,000 members. The Council was much affected in the late 1920's by internal dissensions which for a time precluded regular meetings. William Shaw remained permanent secretary until his death in 1937, when he was succeeded by Arthur Brady (1937-42).

Edinburgh Trades Council became the Trades Council and Labour Party in 1920, and absorbed that of Leith in 1921. It held special conferences in 1922 to promote co-ordination of local trade union effort. It established an industrial committee of seven, for purely trade union activities. Separation of political and industrial sections was frequently sought. The Trades Disputes Act of 1927 necessitated a change in the constitution, but complete separation was avoided, though industrial and political funds were made entirely separate.

EDUCATIONAL AND POLITICAL ACTIVITIES

Some miscellaneous features of the era may be briefly mentioned.

Propaganda for the National Guild movement revived the notion of co-operative production. In Glasgow, a short-lived Building Guild was formed after the war, and undertook municipal contracts, under the leadership of John Winning. A more enduring Tailoring Guild was set up, also in Glasgow, by the Garment Workers Union (1921), as was a Guild promoted by the National Union of Clerks.

Another striking phenomenon was the rent agitation. A Scottish Housing Commission with trade union representatives had been appointed in 1912; it reported in 1917, demonstrating a deficiency of one million houses in Scotland. The shortage was aggravated by the stoppage of building and aggregation of population in certain areas during the war; but in the main it was a heritage of the persistently low standards of accommodation and the overcrowding that had existed in Scotland throughout the industrial period and indeed earlier.

The increase of rents was one of the most resented forms of war profiteering, and was to some extent checked in response to popular pressure, notably a campaign in Govan of resistance to payment of increased charges and to evictions attempted in default. Rent Restriction Acts were passed, and in view of the slow progress of post-war housing schemes, were retained in principle. Their application in certain cases produced agitation and litigation. Tenants' Defence and Housing Associations sprang up, and won a notable triumph in the *Kerr* v. *Bryde* case, conducted by D. D. Cormack for the Clydebank Housing Association, when the Sheriff decided that under the 1920 Act 'notice to quit' was essential before rent could legally be increased. This was affirmed on appeal by the House of Lords (December 1922). The Scottish Labour Housing Association, of which John Wheatley was president and David Kirkwood secretary, issued a manifesto claiming in view of this decision the right to withhold rent. It also campaigned for interest-free public housing loans.

Forward continued to flourish as an independent organ. On becoming a member of the second Labour Government, Johnston was succeeded in the editorship by Emrys Hughes, a son-in-law of Keir Hardie. For six years (February 1925 to 1931) a local weekly *Labour Standard* was published in Edinburgh; it finally succumbed from lack of advertising revenue. Originated independently, it was from October 1927 controlled by a committee on which the Trades Council was represented. *The Edinburgh Free Press*, published by Frank Maitland, was started in November 1934, but was also short-lived.

In Aberdeen and Dundee there were also local organs. The *Dundee Free Press* arose from the general strike and consequent trade union boycott of the local press monopoly. Both this and the similar periodical in Aberdeen continued for a few years. James Leatham, an active publicist who became provost of Turriff in Aberdeenshire, published there independently the monthly *Gateway* for a number of years; it consisted largely of self-written Socialist propaganda. The *Shetlander* was issued as a monthly by the Economics Club in Lerwick. Patrick Dollan contributed a Scottish column to the *Daily Herald.*

The Workers' Educational Association, which had formed a few branches prior to the war, immediately afterwards constituted a district, with a full-time organising secretary, a post first held, till 1927, by Herbert Highton, an engineer, sometime chairman of Glasgow Trades Council. On the formation of the Workers' Educational Trade Union Committee (W.E.T.U.C.), Scotland was provided with a divisional committee, with the same secretary. The Iron and Steel Trades Confederation and the Union of Post Office Workers were the pioneers and chief supporters. Though having the official approval until 1937 of the Scottish T.U.C., and the active collaboration of prominent unionists such as Joseph Duncan of the Farm Servants (for many years chairman) and Charles Gallie of the Railway Clerks, the W.E.A. did not make much headway in the movement, and its activities were largely confined to the Clyde area. The Edinburgh branch seceded in 1926 and became an independent body, which in 1965 changed its name to the Edinburgh Extra-Mural Association. The W.E.A., which later divided into three Scottish districts, collaborated in the formation of Regional Committees for Adult Education, attached to the four Scottish universities, and acquired representatives on the Extra-Mural Committee which these successively established.

The Scottish Labour College, founded in Glasgow at a conference in March 1917, was at first distinctly left-wing in sympathy, with John Maclean as full-time tutor. It became part of the National Council of Labour Colleges, which set up two districts in Scotland, with full-time officers, of whom Charles Gibbons was long active in the Edinburgh area. The national body was for some time run from Edinburgh, under the secretaryship of James P. M. Millar; it was transferred to London in 1927 and removed to Tillicoultry as a war emergency measure in 1940, and remained there. In 1924-25 it had affiliations from five Scottish and eight national unions, and arrangements with several others; over 800 local working-class bodies were associated with it. It tended to become more 'orthodox' and to seek close association with the official Labour movement; its national president, Arthur Woodburn, became Scottish Secretary of the Labour Party, and was Secretary for Scotland in the third Labour Government. It secured the support of some of the most influential unions, such as Miners, Railwaymen and Distributive Workers. A residential college at 13 Burnbank Gardens, with a four-month course of day classes at a fee of £5, was commenced in the winter of 1919, but soon abandoned. Effort was concentrated on evening courses and weekend schools, and a large variety of lectures was conducted chiefly with the aid of voluntary tutors; a number of these were schoolmasters or possessed of other academic qualifications.

As regards political action, seven Labour members were elected in Scotland at the 'coupon' election of December 1918. G. N. Barnes, member of the War Cabinet, and former secretary of A.S.E., was repudiated by the Party, but retained his seat against the officially endorsed but extremely independent John Maclean. A few candidates were unsuccessfully nominated by the National Democratic Labour Party, composed chiefly of ex-Labour supporters of the Lloyd-George Government; David Gilmour, once secretary of the Lanarkshire Miners, was its secretary.

The election of 1922 had sensational results, seven seats being won in Glasgow, making ten out of a total of fifteen; in sum, thirty were elected in Scotland. The election of 1923 showed a slight further rise to thirty-four; the 'Zinoviev' election of 1924 brought a net loss of eight. There was recovery at by-elections, and an increase to thirty-six in 1929. Severe losses—a reduction to seven—occurred in the 'save the pound' election of 1931; there was recovery to twenty-two, together with three of the now disaffiliated I.L.P. in 1935.

The first two Labour Governments, of 1923-24 and 1929-31, though presided over by the Scot Ramsay MacDonald, who owed his leadership largely to the support of his fellow-countrymen, contained few Scottish members. Apart from Lord Haldane, a late recruit from Liberalism, as Lord Chancellor, and William Adamson, who had been the first post-war leader in the Commons, as Secretary for Scotland, the only Scot in the Cabinet was John Wheatley, whose housing policy won his repute as an administrator. William Graham of Edinburgh, a journalist with academic training, similarly won favour at the Board of Trade in the second ministry; his premature death, soon after, was a great loss. Whether or not due to the inertia of Adamson, Scottish affairs were neglected under both regimes. Hence in part the stimulus to Scottish Nationalism, some of whose protagonists, such as the veterans Cunninghame Graham, G. B. Clark and Roland Muirhead, professed Socialist views. An independent political party was formed in 1928, and reconstituted as the Scottish National Party in 1934.

It appears that the industrial working-class vote, which had been steadily given to the Liberal Party until 1914, had gone over almost *en masse* to Labour; whether the explanation lies mainly in the disruption and decadence of its old party, economic changes, especially the post-war depression, or in the vigour of Socialist propaganda in the 'twenties, requires further analysis. At any rate, there seems to have been little change of outlook in many cases, but fundamentally opposition to the Conservative Party. The Irish vote was, on the whole, favourable to official Labour, though in some instances, e.g. Motherwell, inclined to a rather incongruous alliance with Communism. The Party of the latter registered its solitary Scottish gains with Walton Newbold in that constituency (1922-23) and William Gallacher in West Fife, at the expense of Adamson, in 1935. Its adherents were excluded from the Scottish Labour Party Conference in February 1923; and in terms of the British Labour Party Conference decision were debarred from acting as officials in or delegates from affiliated bodies (1935). Originally constituted after the war by members of the British Socialist Party, Left members of the I.L.P. and a few other groups, it became an integral part of the Communist International, and attracted a number of supporters, many of them transiently. Members were active in the Unemployed Workers Peace Council and other Left organisations.

John Maclean, *plus communiste que les communistes*, with a few admirers carried on, until his early death, propaganda for a Scottish Workers' Republican Party and issued the monthly *Vanguard*. The Londoner Guy Aldred settled in Glasgow after the war, established a bookshop, and published the monthly *Word* and numerous pamphlets in advocacy of anarchism.

The I.L.P. had over 200 branches in Scotland by the end of the war, and carried on active propaganda. It was responsible for a majority of the Labour candidatures in the elections of the 'twenties, and most of those elected were members. Dissatisfaction with the official policy became acute during the administration of 1929-31, and its downfall was soon followed by a definite split. The Disaffiliationists claimed the name and property of the old body, and retained some strength in the west, reflected in Parliamentary and municipal representation, and partly due to the personality and popularity of James Maxton. The affiliationists took the name of the Scottish Socialist Party (1932), under the guidance of Patrick J. Dollan, but it was uninfluential and short-lived. The Divisional Labour Parties, which now sometimes had strong 'individual membership sections' generally superseded the older local bodies.

The National Labour Party, formed by supporters of MacDonald after the crisis of 1931, also had little support in Scotland. John Davidson, an Edinburgh veteran, was prominent in it; Craigie Aitchison, the Lord Advocate, alone in Scotland retained office and his seat; he was soon raised to the Bench. The only Scottish M.P. to adhere, temporarily, to the Mosley secession was Robert Forgan, a Glasgow doctor and councillor, son of an ex-Moderator. He and a few other 'New Party' candidates polled negligibly at the General Election of 1931.

The Scottish Fabian Societies held annual conferences and were accorded one representative on the Scottish Council of the Labour Party; an over-elaborate federal constitution was adopted in 1938. Dr. Drummond Shiels and Robert Gibson, K.C., who both held minor Government offices, were among the best-known members. The re-christened Social Democratic Federation retained a few loyal adherents, including one M.P., Thomas Kennedy, who won Kirkcaldy at a by-election (1921). In Glasgow the Study Circle, founded by the Quaker, Robert Shanks, provided a forum for the advocates of Christian socialism and pacifism.

The Scottish Co-operative Union in April 1917 approved by a large majority the formation of a Joint Advisory Committee with the Trade Union and Labour organisations; and in subsequent elections the Co-operative Party sponsored a few candidatures, in collaboration with the local Labour Party, including Thomas Henderson, elected for Tradeston (Glasgow) in 1922.

Glasgow Labour in 1919 held 19 seats on the City Council; this was increased to 44 at a 'general election' consequent on the extension of the city boundaries in 1920. After a period of alternate gains and losses, a majority, dependent on I.L.P. support, was obtained in 1934, when the first Labour Lord Provost was appointed; he was the veteran John Stewart, and was succeeded in 1938 by P. J. Dollan and in 1941 by John M. Biggar (1875-1943), an accountant, who four times contested Paisley. Earlier examples of Labour majorities were afforded in the small burghs of Cumnock, Dalkeith, Kirkintilloch and Kilsyth. In Dundee a slender majority was held for a year. Labour generally fared badly in the 'proportional representation' elections to the short-lived Local Education Authorities, where in industrial areas sectarianism was rampant; and save in the Clyde valley and in Fife had meagre representation on the county councils, even after they were raised into prominence and power by the far-reaching Local Government Act of 1929.

In summary, it may be said that the period falls into two fairly distinct divisions. The 'twenties were years of militancy, industrial strife and rapid acquisition of political power, amid economic depression. The 'thirties, amid some economic recovery, witnessed a political standstill, a decline of propaganda, and latterly preoccupation with the international situation rather than internal problems. In the industrial sphere, there were predominantly peaceful relations, and the official adoption of a policy of collaborationism. This was stigmatised by critics as one of compromise if not betrayal, but was defended as a tactic justified by circumstances, and sometimes exalted as appropriate to a new stage of economic evolution, one in which trade unionism, having attained recognition of its independent rights, was proceeding to partnership as an essential element in the constitution of society.

Chapter VII

EPILOGUE: THE SECOND WORLD WAR AND AFTER

Contemporary history is always difficult to write, owing both to abundance of material and lack of perspective; that of the Scottish Labour movement is peculiarly so, because of its increased involvement in that of Britain.

During the Second World War, the political and industrial sections gave official support to Government war policy; an electoral truce was proclaimed. Hostility to Fascism and Nazi repression of trade unionism and socialism, increasing in the 'thirties, facilitated this attitude. Opposition was confined to the small remnant of the I.L.P. under James Maxton, and to the Communists, until the entry of U.S.S.R. into the war, after which they became its most enthusiastic protagonists. Labour acceptance of office in the National Government was generally approved, and the administration of Thomas Johnston as Secretary for Scotland gained general appreciation. Towards the end of the war, some criticism of internal rather than war policy emerged, and independent candidates, running sometimes as spokesmen of the Commonwealth group of Richard Acland, polled well; the Scottish Nationalists won a seat in the spring of 1945.

Trade union membership grew rapidly, with the approximation to full employment, and nearly doubled between 1939 and 1947, when it reached almost 700,000. Unions affiliated to the Scottish Trade Union Congress rose to 83, and Trades Councils to 51; unions of a professional type, such as the Association of Scientific Workers, were among those recruited. A Youth Advisory Council was formed in 1941, and annual conferences of this and of the Women's Advisory Council (1927) were held; their reports were submitted to and included in the annual report of Congress. The total female membership was over 120,000. For the former federal structure was substituted, after long negotiations, in 1944 a National Union of Scottish Mineworkers, which next year became an integral party of the newly constituted National Union of Mineworkers. In 1942, the Building and

Monumental Workers' Association of Scotland transferred engagements to the Amalgamated Union of Building Trade Workers of Great Britain. About twenty independent Scottish unions survived, mainly in building and textiles; the Bakers and Typographical Unions were among the largest.

Several of the older generation of trade union leaders died during this period, including Robert Smillie of the Miners, Thomas Barron of the Builders, John Syme of the Jute Workers, James Walker of the Iron and Steel Trades and William G. Hunter of the Bakers. Trade union representatives served on numerous wartime government committees; the S.T.U.C. reaffiliated to the W.E.A. (1944), and was associated with the Scottish Council on Industry and the Scottish Council of Social Service, formed in 1943.

The end of the war in Europe produced a rapid change in the political situation. Labour representatives withdrew from the Government, and in the election of 1945 the Labour Party asserted its independence. Scotland returned 37 Labour members, together with three members of the I.L.P. and one Communist (William Gallacher). It was not, however, so well represented in the first majority Labour government of 1945-51 as in its short-lived predecessors. Thomas Johnston retired from politics to serve on the North of Scotland Hydro-Electric Board and in other non-party public activities. His successors at the Scottish Office commanded less esteem, seeming to share the now general attitude of the Party, that the previously recognised special grievances and claims of Scotland would be eliminated by Labour rule. Some minor administrative devolution was conceded. The S.T.U.C. from 1950 also disassociated itself from the demand for greater autonomy—hence considerable criticism from Nationalist groups, divided as to the extent of self-government which they advocated. Scottish National Congress, led by a veteran of the early Scottish Labour Party, Roland Muirhead, combined championship of Socialism with that of Home Rule.

With the death in 1946 of James Maxton, whose personal appeal had largely held its members together, the I.L.P. became insignificant, and lost representation in Parliament, as did the Communists. Guy Aldred until his death in 1964, through publication of the monthly *Word* and numerous propagandist pamphlets, proclaimed the Anarchist gospel in Glasgow.

The Conservative triumph in three successive General Elections was not so marked in Scotland, where the Labour Party maintained its strength. Left-wing criticism, especially of the apparent retreat from nationalisation, and even more of the alleged bipartisan subordination to U.S.A. foreign policy, was vocal; the latter was expressed in support of unilateral nuclear disarmament and participation in demonstrations against bases, e.g. in South Uist and the Holy Loch. Unity was however preserved in the electoral field; approved candidates were predominantly of the Right, Emrys Hughes, son-in-law and political heir of Keir Hardie, being a privileged exception.

There was some revival of the Liberal Party, which for example declared its independence of the dominant Progressives in Edinburgh municipal affairs. Labour retained a large majority in Glasgow, and a smaller one in both Aberdeen and Dundee, while controlling several smaller burghs and a few county councils in the industrial areas; it at length made some progress towards equality in Edinburgh.

The Liberal revival, especially in the rural areas, aided by such factors as general opposition to the 'Beeching Plan', which proposed drastic curtailment of the Scottish railways, contributed to the Tory defeat in the election of autumn 1964. The new Government, with *novi homines* in office, included in its programme—inspired by Keynesian economics rather than Socialist idealism—plans for the amelioration of Scotland's economic position, national and regional, especially the Highlands.

The parlous condition of the Scottish economy in the inter-war period, somewhat relieved in the later 'thirties, and temporarily overcome by war demand, did not recur, though economic growth was proportionately half, and unemployment frequently double that south of the Border. Loss of jobs tended to be concentrated in certain areas, due to such factors as the virtual cessation of native shale-oil mining and the discontinuance of the manufacture of conventional arms. The introduction of new industries, often American controlled, was facilitated by the extended provision of industrial estates and other aid for the widely expanded 'Development Areas' and by the Local Employment Acts. Agriculture generally prospered under a complex system of public assistance. 'New towns' were created, at East Kilbride,

Glenrothes and Cumbernauld; Grangemouth was the chief example of more spontaneous expansion as a 'boom town'.

Under these circumstances, under both Labour and Tory rule, the trade union movement officially continued a collaborationist policy, though 'unofficial' strikes were frequent, notably in nationalised mining and transport. The former claims to 'workers' control', or even participation in management were abandoned in the setting up of 'public corporations' to administer nationalised industries and services. The trade union movement generally rejected workers' representation on their Boards for fear of compromising independence. A few larger scale strikes arose, mainly from demarcation disputes, friction among unions rather than with the employer, or the maintenance of differential wage rates. The trend to incorporation in all-British unions continued. Membership in Scotland was estimated at over 900,000. The strength of trade unionism lay in the metal-working, building, commerce and distribution and miscellaneous groups, the first of these accounting for one-fifth of the total. About one-half of membership is concentrated in the Clyde conurbation. The Horse and Motormen and the Bakers were among the largest purely Scottish unions. 'Recognition' was normal; the protracted and publicised contrary policy of D. C. Thomson of Dundee was the subject of a court of inquiry in 1952.

The Scottish T.U.C. remained an active body, though it lost its able secretary William Elger (1891-1946) shortly after the war, and one of its most noted leaders on the retirement of Joseph F. Duncan (1879-1965), of the Farm Servants. In 1957 it reported the affiliation of 91 unions, with over three-quarters of a million members. Its spokesmen were prominent in the Scottish Council for Development and Industry which issued constructive proposals for economic advance, notably in the Toothill Report of 1960. The S.T.U.C. Council arbitrated in several inter-union disputes. It was critical of some aspects of Labour Government policy, such as the restriction of social services in 1951. A trend to the Left was more manifest by 1961, both in home and foreign policy.

The Trades Councils, confining themselves to the industrial field, left political activities to the local Labour Parties, as in Edinburgh (1951). Edinburgh (1959) and Glasgow (1958) Councils celebrated their official centenaries, and published historical brochures. Edinburgh in 1964 acquired up-to-date premises, with fully-equipped club facilities.

The co-operative movement continued its commercial success; a notable example was the pioneering by the S.C.W.S. of retail trade in the Highlands; ventures in hotel keeping and holiday agencies were also made. Some amalgamation of local societies took place, especially in the Glasgow area. Union with the Co-operative Wholesale Society in England was more than once rejected. In 1958, there were reckoned to be 171 societies, with a membership approaching one and a half million.

In the educational sphere the National Council of Labour Colleges, which removed its headquarters during the war to Tillicoultry, devoted itself primarily to technical education in trade unionism and similar matters. The Workers' Educational Association was reorganised in three Scottish Districts, and collaborated with the Extra-Mural Departments which by 1965 were established in all the then four Scottish universities (now increased in number). In 1964-65 a scheme came into operation whereby educational provision for trade unions was taken over by the T.U.C., and the activities of the N.C.L.C. and the Trade Union Committee of the W.E.A. were superseded.

Paradoxically, in the period of economic and political growth, an independent Labour press has almost disappeared. *Forward* was taken over by the Labour Party as an official organ, but was shortly discontinued, as was the *Daily Herald*, with some circulation in Scotland, in which the T.U.C. for some time held a part interest. The *Edinburgh Clarion*, founded during the war by West Edinburgh D.L.P., also soon failed under official auspices.

Divisional Labour Parties were established and maintained throughout the constituencies, but were largely inactive, except at elections; even then, whether due to the vogue of wireless and television, or to a general apathy and inertia, meetings were relatively ill-attended, in sharp contrast with the enthusiasm of the 'twenties. Thus propaganda, whether by the spoken or the printed word, declined; Fabian Societies in a few centres served as almost its only organ, speaking to the converted few.

The trend to the 'corporative' or 'managerial' society, characterised by large-scale centralisation and bureaucratic administration, both public and private, which is common to all western countries, together with the achievement of the 'Age of Affluence' and the Welfare State, have blunted the edge of the working-class movement. Whether the present social and economic order will survive the risk of nuclear war and the longer term stress of diminishing natural resources and increasing population in the world is a theme for the prophet rather than the historian.

BIBLIOGRAPHY

As stated in the Foreword, a very full list of material, published and unpublished, is contained in the *Bibliography of the Scottish Working Class Movement*, edited by Ian MacDougall (1965).

Much of the present study is based on unpublished records of trade unions and other bodies, on Government reports and on periodicals. A select list of these main sources is appended. Detailed references are cited in my articles in the *Economic History Review* (April 1935) and the *International Review of Social History* (1938); and in the relevant sections of my books *Economic Developments in Victorian Scotland* (1937) and *Scotland in Modern Times* (1964). These, and Professor R. H. Campbell's *Scotland since 1707* (1965) also elaborate the economic and social background of the Labour movement.

Minutes of Edinburgh Trades Council.

Minutes of Scottish Miners Federation.

Reports of Scottish Trades Union Congress.

Files of *True Scotsman* (1838-41), *Glasgow Sentinel* (1850-77), *Glasgow Echo* (1893-95), *Forward* (1906 *et seq.*), *Glasgow Herald* and *Scotsman* (*passim*).

J. L. Gray, *Law of Combination in Scotland* (*Economica*, December 1928).

T. Johnston, *History of Working Classes in Scotland* (1920).

R. W. Postgate, *The Builders' History* (1923).

S. Gillespie, *A Hundred Years of Progress: the Scottish Typographical Association* (1953).

R. P. Arnot, *The Scottish Miners* (1955).

W. Diack, *The Trades Council and Trade Union Movement in Aberdeen* (1939).

K. C. Buckley, *Trade Unionism in Aberdeen*, 1878-1900 (1955).

L. C. Wright, *Scottish Chartism* (1953).

D. Lowe, *Souvenirs of Scottish Labour* (1918).

W. Stewart, *Keir Hardie* (1921).

E. Hughes, *Keir Hardie* (1956).

Reports of Select Committee on Artisans (1824), Select Committee on the Combination Laws (1825), Select Committee on Master and Servant (1865); Reports of Commissioners on Trade Unions (1867-69); Reports of Royal Commissions on Depression of Trade and Industry (1886), and on Labour (1892-94).

INDEX